Brief Lives:
Wilkie Collins

Brief Lives:
Wilkie Collins

Melisa Klimaszewski

Brief Lives
Published by Hesperus Press Limited
19 Bulstrode Street, London W1U 2JN
www.hesperuspress.com

First published by Hesperus Press Limited, 2011

Designed and typeset by Fraser Muggeridge studio
Printed in Jordan by Jordan National Press

ISBN: 978-1-84391-915-5

Contents

Introduction

Wilkie Collins' first published book was a biography. He begins the first chapter with these words: 'To write biography successfully, is to present the truth under its most instructive and agreeable aspect.' Agreeability certainly ranks high among the goals of this volume in the *Brief Lives* series, but rather than ensuring that Wilkie Collins himself always appears agreeable, this biography prioritises making the reading experience pleasant. In framing his attempt as a biographer, Collins perhaps encourages those who will write of his life to find lessons in his experiences, but his instruction raises the question: what is the 'truth' of one's life? Many individuals struggle to answer that question personally, and it presents even more complications when asked about the life of another. 'Truth' is the most slippery of terms, depending for its existence upon point of view, historical distance and context. Modern biographers are increasingly comfortable with the notion of multiple truths, accepting the impossibility of constructing a single, authoritative narrative of a life.

Writing a brief biography of a man whose life was hardly short presents additional challenges. Which events are the most significant? Which friendships merit the lengthiest examination? How deeply to contemplate each literary work and the culture of which it formed a part? In the pages that follow, I attempt to balance attention to these matters as I reconstruct a sense of

Collins' personal character, discussing his life's work in a manner that encourages further inquiry. Since most brief summations of a famous figure's career tend to focus on celebrated writings, I have intentionally counterbalanced that trend by discussing some of Collins' lesser-known works in a fair amount of detail. The less popular fiction contains surprisingly compelling views of Collins as a storyteller, and my treatment of those texts aims to supplement the more widely available analyses of Collins' more frequently studied works. In some cases, notably for *The Woman in White* and *The Moonstone*, I have refrained from revealing complete plot details that would spoil the surprises of a first reading. In addition to his fiction, several aspects of Collins' life – his friendships; the artistic movements in which he and his friends participated; his entrance into debates about nineteenth-century medicine, psychology, science and race – will be fascinating for interested readers to investigate in more detail. This volume, then, endeavours not only to provide a substantial amount of information about Collins but also to offer fresh insights into his work and to serve as a valuable starting point for additional studies of his life, his writing and the era in which he lived.

To facilitate a streamlined reading experience, the *Brief Lives* series minimises endnotes. The information in the following chapters comes from a wide range of primary as well as secondary sources, listed in the Bibliography. I am joined by other Collins scholars in my debt to Catherine Peters' *The King of Inventors: A Life of Wilkie Collins*, an authoritative and excellent full-length biography that makes extensive use of Harriet Collins' as yet unpublished journal and contains a wealth of information about Collins' childhood. Lyn Pykett's *Wilkie Collins* in Oxford's *Authors in Context* series, William Clarke's *The Secret Life of Wilkie Collins*, and Andrew Gasson's *Wilkie Collins: An Illustrated Guide* have also been very helpful sources. I cannot overstate the value of two reference works: William Baker's *A Wilkie Collins Chronology* and *The Public Face of Wilkie*

Collins, four volumes of Collins' collected letters edited by William Baker, Andrew Gasson, Graham Law and Paul Lewis. *The Public Face* makes many of Collins' letters available to a wide readership for the first time, and the editors provide detailed information for other letters that appear in *The Letters of Wilkie Collins*, two volumes edited by William Baker and William M. Clarke. For each of Collins' letters cited in the following chapters, I have provided a full date, which enables one to find the letter in either *The Public Face* or *The Letters*. Letters written by Charles Dickens appear in the twelve-volume Oxford Pilgrim Edition of *The Letters of Charles Dickens*. Marks of emphasis, such as underlining, in quoted letters appear in the original documents.

Wilkie Collins wrote all manner of fiction – detective stories, sensation novels, ghost stories, domestic dramas – full of surprises and mysteries to be solved. His life was also full of sensational elements that may startle readers who imagine Victorians as uncomplicated bodies sipping tea at lace-laden tables while dutifully devoting their souls to domestic firesides. Raised by pious evangelical parents in a stable family and taught to appreciate fine art as well as literature, Collins comes from a background that points to the status quo. One may look to him as the author of several best-selling novels expecting to see examples of Victorian tradition. What one finds in Collins' life as well as his work, however, are endless instances of behaviours, perspectives and values that are anything but simple or conventional. Instead, one discovers questioning, complication, ambiguity and outright challenges to dominant cultural norms. Collins' novels often privilege the points of view of outsiders or misfits, and he refused to live in a conventional domestic marriage. Yet his fame and the popularity of his work continued to grow in his lifetime, and his circle of friends included the most famous of fellow writers and artists. In Collins, then, one finds a life remarkable not only for what it reveals about an accomplished and intriguing author, but also for the way it causes us to re-evaluate what we associate with the term Victorian. More dynamic than static, Victorian culture tolerated and sometimes even welcomed subversive figures, among whose voices Collins' occasionally arose loudest.

– *Melisa Klimaszewski*

From Willie to Wilkie

On 8th January 1824, Harriet Collins gave birth to her first child, William Wilkie Collins, in what was then the northwest London neighbourhood of Marylebone. The healthy, light-haired baby boy was born with a noticeable physical irregularity: a large bulge on the right side of his forehead. The firm protuberance, looking something like a tennis ball trying to press its way out of his cranium, is visible in depictions spanning Collins' life, from an early sketch of him as an infant to photographs of the elderly Collins. These images show not a grotesque, shocking deformity but rather an insistent and unmasked oddity on a large forehead. Photographs of Collins as an adult show his hair combed back – no awkward attempts to spread his front locks over the bulge and no turning to one side to mask it.

The forehead peculiarity immediately marked the boy, whose first nickname was Willie, as unusual. Although he was sensitive about the irregularities in his appearance and the large size of his head, a sense of being different from others did not traumatise him. Having such a temperament was most fortunate for the young man because, as he matured, his extremities did not keep pace with the rest of his growing body. His hands and feet remained extremely tiny. Searching for shoes and boots, Collins often sought sizes smaller than the average woman's, and he could slip into items made for young children. These challenges, though, did not cause Collins to long for normalcy. He admired those with more ideal physical forms, but he did not develop an intense or bitter desire to fit in with the masses. In fact, from a young age, Collins was comfortable confronting and disputing social custom.

In his distaste for traditional mores, young Willie could not have differed more from his father, who highly valued proper appearances and social acceptance. William Collins, born 18th September 1788, sought a type of artistic success that was linked to entry in elite circles. The son of a Scotswoman and an Irishman settled in England, William Collins sold paintings to provide a key source of income after his father died bankrupt in 1812. The senior William Collins had been an art dealer and freelance journalist whose abolitionist work 'The Slave Trade: A Poem Written in 1788' inspired his friend George Morland to compose a painting of the same name that was exhibited at the Royal Academy. Eventually, the junior William Collins would also find patrons at the very top of Victorian society. In 1818, the Prince Regent bought Collins' *Scene on the Coast of Norfolk*, and Collins became a Royal Academician in 1820.

With a stable career and income, William could now consider marrying a beautiful Scottish woman whom he had admired for years: Harriet Geddes. Harriet and William met at a small artists' ball in Edinburgh in 1814, when neither deemed it practical to pursue a romance. They bumped into one another every couple of years, but it was not until a chance meeting in London in 1821 that Collins intensified the relationship. Now they courted as two adults, mature in their love and in their acknowledgment of financial as well as familial obstacles. She had no dowry, and his mother wanted to delay the match because of worries about William's financial stability. The circumstances surrounding the actual marriage are interesting. On 16th September 1822, the two married in Scotland, where William was travelling as part of the entourage surrounding George IV's official visit. Wilkie Collins' biography of his father states that the couple wed in Scotland to place themselves well away from the objections of William's mother. The unpopular Marriage Act of 1822, repealed after its stipulations had been in effect for just seven months, prevented a couple from marrying over parental opposition. The provisions of the Act, though, did not come into effect until 1st September 1822, which leaves one wondering why the couple had not simply taken vows in England earlier.

William expressed especially ardent concern about Harriet making a trip to Edinburgh by herself in a letter from 24th August 1822. He suggests that the trip might be manageable with a protective escort, then writes, 'And yet, I feel so nervous at the idea of your journey in your present state of health, and without *me*, that I am quite miserable.' Why, after a prolonged courtship, did the couple suddenly feel compelled to wed during William's trip? What motivated William to underscore that his companionship was most appropriate at this particular time? It seems most peculiar, after over seven years of patience, to hasten the nuptials with Harriet in a fragile 'state of health'. Although Wilkie, quoting this letter in *Memoirs of William Collins*, would not have aimed at raising questions about his parents' earlier chastity, it is at least possible that Harriet's health was affected by a pregnancy that did not result in a healthy birth. William hoped in the same letter that a consecrated union might 'brighten our present prospects'. The marriage was not scandalised by its association with Scotland, the site of many elopements due to its more permissive marriage laws, but the couple, for whatever reason, was certainly eager in the autumn of 1822 to seal their union officially.

By nineteenth-century standards, Harriet Geddes married herself out of a state of spinsterhood at the age of thirty-two. Her younger sister Margaret had wed previously, and Harriet had overcome the challenge of finding a way to support herself financially in a society that closed professions to women. The eldest child of Harriet Easton and Alexander William Reynolds Geddes, Harriet sought employment after her father, a former army officer, experienced a financial downfall. She nearly began a career as a theatre actress, which would have placed her forever outside the realm of genteel social circles. Displaying their bodies on stage for pay and calling deliberate attention to themselves, actresses were presumed to have relaxed morals and were often likened to prostitutes. Harriet's enjoyment of plays was rekindled later in life through her son's theatrical pursuits, but in her youth, it was replaced with governessing. Funded by a concerned evangelical, Harriet pursued studies that enabled her to work as a schoolmistress before securing posts as a private governess for several years, not only supporting herself but also helping to bolster her family's finances. Once Harriet married William Collins and left governessing, she showed no desire to pursue employment or studies of her own; indeed, she disapproved of many women who focused on non-domestic pursuits. Cultivating an interest in stage performance as the young wife of an increasingly respected artist would have been out of the question.

Harriet's sister Margaret, who took the name Carpenter in marriage and had eight children, did continue a more public career as the family's reputation continued to rise in the art world. Margaret impressively displayed portraits at the Royal Academy, where women were denied official membership, for over half a century. Her talent garnered critical praise as well as loyal patrons, and several of her works are in the National Portrait Gallery. William Collins' work continued to impress the Prince Regent, who commissioned another piece, *Prawn Fishers at Hastings* (completed in 1825), after he assumed the throne as King George IV. *The Highland Girl* (1818), a portrait of Samuel Taylor Coleridge's daughter Sara, was widely admired, and Collins was also friendly with Coleridge's close collaborator, William Wordsworth, who would later become Poet Laureate. The famous Scottish painter, David Wilkie, was such a close friend that Collins chose to embed him in the family tree by using his surname for the middle name of his firstborn. Multiple lines of family history, then, on the maternal as well as the paternal side, pointed in artistic directions for young Willie, but he was not the son who would be known for continuing the family's painting legacy.

Four years after Willie's birth, Harriet and William welcomed another son into the family: Charles Allston Collins, born 25th January 1828. As Willie's middle name honoured an artist, Charley's paid tribute to Washington Allston, an American painter who studied at the Royal Academy Schools, was a close friend of Coleridge, and spent several years in Italy as well as England. Delicate and sickly for most of his life, Charley developed a more reserved and less confident personality than his older brother, but they were good friends. Each tried his hand at painting, often under the shadow of their father's brush, with Charley's work showing the most promise. The close-knit family spent much of their time together and, when separated, corresponded faithfully. In a letter from William to Harriet from 17th October 1831, William transcribes messages from each boy. Willie's shows not only how central epistles were to maintaining ties with extended family but also a bit of a silly streak: 'I have had a letter from my Aunt Christy which was put in one for you, it made us all laugh uncle George putting a message in your letter that he was a monkey.'

Like most families in their social class, the Collinses employed domestic servants, and it would not have been abnormal for the boys to spend more time with a nursemaid and a tutor than with their own mother. Harriet, however, was a solicitous and involved parent who taught her sons their lessons and tended them carefully when they were ill. She remained a convivial person, but her love of entertaining would not emerge strongly again until her widowhood. In the meantime, she directed her energies towards her children and enforced regular attendance at church, which Willie disliked. Collins recalled witnessing demonstrations at the age of eight in support of the First Reform Bill in 1832. Even though the Collinses were Tories who did not suppport the reforms, they illuminated all of their home's windows to repel the stones of protesters. While the reforms of 1832 did not please those hoping for true equality, which was deemed a radical demand, the changes to the law did increase representation in Parliament. A redistribution of seats increased representation for urban areas, and a few hundred thousand more men out of twenty-four million could vote, but one still had to own property in order to choose one's parliamentary representative. Even such limited reforms did not appeal to William Collins' sentiments, and his family's life revolved in large part around instilling proper Tory values in the boys.

The Collins household was strictly Protestant, and William firmly observed Sunday as the Sabbath. He was dismayed when he noticed others breaking the sanctity of the day with labour or diversion, and his letters showcase the centrality of worship to his and Harriet's marriage. When William travelled, often for several weeks at a time, he expressed a longing for his wife. In a letter of 2nd October 1828, he wrote, 'I could go on for an hour describing our blessings; but your heart is not insensible to the merits of Providence, and when I return, we will thank our heavenly Father together' (*Memoirs* Vol I, 313–4). Collins sweetly anticipated the long-delayed resumption of a physical, and presumably conjugal, embrace alongside the return of joint prayer.

William did not enjoy the long separations from his family that his travel to paint landscapes or to complete commissioned portraits occasioned, so the family began to travel together. Harriet's elderly and weak mother had resided with the family since Charley's infancy, and she joined the Collinses' trip abroad in the summer of 1829. For six weeks, when Willie was five years old and Charley nearing a year and a half, the family went to Boulogne. Perhaps fuelled by Harriet's outgoing and curious disposition, the family took more trips after her mother's death in December of 1833, spending the months of June to September of 1834 in Wales. Willie did well upon his enrolment at the Maida

Hill Academy in January of 1835, but further travel would educate him far more thoroughly than his classroom experiences.

The most formative period of Wilkie Collins' adolescence, by his own account, began in September of 1836 when his parents moved the family to Italy. For two years, living abroad led Willie to discover new worlds of sights, sounds, tastes, and attitudes. Later in life, Collins emphasised how important the experience was to the formation of his character. On the family's way to Rome, they were of course exposed to other places on the continent, and two weeks spent in Paris brought surprises. Harriet and William were appalled at the moral laxity they saw in Parisians and disliked French cooking, but young Willie was intrigued and stimulated. He would form a lifelong love of French food, speak the language and visit the country often as an adult. The Collinses also saw Marseilles, Cannes and Nice, where they spent six weeks waiting for a cholera epidemic in Italy to pass. The delay was unwelcome and the disease outbreak worrisome, but the respite somewhat stabilised the travel-weary family. In Nice, Charley (who had become ill in Marseilles) could recuperate without constant movement, Willie was schooled by a young Jewish tutor, and the family could regularly attend services at an English church. William Collins' continued frustration with the travel delays, however, led him to take the uncharacteristically risky decision of moving his family towards Italy based on sketchy news from a friend that the quarantine was an overreaction and that travel was safe.

Descending in awe from the magnificent Alps in early December, the family rested in Genoa. A harsh winter storm and more bouts of illness for Harriet and Charley hampered their enjoyment of Florence, where they arrived on Christmas Eve, and slowed their remaining travel, but they finally reached Rome on 7th January 1837. Although Harriet and William socialised with fellow British residents and visitors, avoiding assimilation to an Italian lifestyle, they did expose their sons to the city's cultural offerings. Willie and Charley witnessed elaborate Holy Week festivities, saw the Colosseum, went to races and operas, and visited the Sistine Chapel. They resided near the Pincian Hill, a spot whose beauty Collins never forgot. While his father worked in a borrowed studio and mingled with other British artists – painters as well as writers, including William Wordsworth – Willie learned to read, write, and speak Italian. He loved the language, the food, the art, and the sight of Roman landscapes as well as Roman women. Collins later boasted to friends about his exploits with a married woman whom he claimed to have seduced in his first 'love adventure'.[1] Returning sixteen years later as an adult, Wilkie explained in a letter to Charley that the Italian scenes had been constantly present in his psyche: 'nothing has astonished me more than my own vivid remembrance of every street and building in this wonderful and mournful place. Houses, fountains, public buildings, shops even appeal to me as familiar objects, that I cannot help fancying I must have been in daily contact with, since my first introduction to them in the old bye gone time' (13th November 1853).

In May of 1837, the Collinses went to Naples, but another cholera outbreak (the warnings of which William thought alarmist and therefore ignored) hastened them on to Sorrento, where they passed several pleasant weeks until William fell ill with severe rheumatic pain. It is worth noting the sort of pain that debilitated William, particularly in light of the ailments that would plague his eldest son later in life. According to Wilkie's memoir of his father, William experienced severe pain in his entire right arm, his left leg joints, and both of his eyes. When all treatments failed to relieve his disabling discomfort, he tried warm sulphur baths in Ischia, a nearby island. To the family's relief, William began to improve, and in early November, they all returned to Naples. Quickly, though, nearly the entire family descended back into ill health, with Willie developing a terrible rash that his father then caught. Charley quite literally fell ill when a playfellow pushed him off a wall on New Year's Eve; the nine-year-old began 1838 with a broken arm.

Having returned to Rome for three months (from February to April), William then took the family on another sightseeing trip through the country, including stops in Florence and Venice, before heading back to England through Austria, Germany and Holland. Back in London by mid-August, the now well-travelled clan settled into a house near Regent's Park, and Willie returned to formal schooling at a boarding establishment in Highbury, north London, managed by a Reverend Cole. The fourteen-year-old's letters home, sometimes written in Italian, registered many complaints. Whether because of the worldly tastes he had acquired abroad, or his small size and somewhat strange appearance, he was persecuted by a boy who would whip him if he did not agree to tell stories before bed. Recalling this time as a torturous period, Collins nonetheless credited the development of his storytelling skill to his experiences with the dreaded bully. Unlike childhood traumas that cause their sufferers to avoid any reminders of the initial events, this forced storytelling resulted in a lifelong enjoyment of the act for Collins. Never happy at the school, receiving a mediocre education, and frequently disciplined by the headmaster, Willie persevered for a little over two years, leaving by the end of 1840.

An uncertain future faced Willie once he quit school. While he debated which occupation would define him, he increasingly used Wilkie as the name that would define him. Edward Antrobus, a family friend whose children William Collins had painted, agreed to provide Wilkie with an informal apprenticeship at the offices of his tea importing firm. At Antrobus & Co., Wilkie was displeased with his clerical assignments, but he remained employed with the tea merchant for more than five years. William Collins tried repeatedly to use his connections to procure a civil service position for Wilkie, but the efforts ended fruitlessly. One thing that did recommend Antrobus & Co. was its proximity to the offices of so many major publications, including *Punch*, *The Illustrated London News*, *The Saturday Magazine*, and the publishing house of Chapman and Hall, one of Charles

Dickens' publishers. Antrobus was also generous in permitting Collins to take long travelling holidays. When he had to remain at the office, he spent most of his time writing stories, which began to appear anonymously in journals like *Bentley's Miscellany*, while Charley continued to demonstrate that he had inherited more of his father's talent in the visual arts.

In the summer of 1842, despite poor health and a recent diagnosis of heart disease on top of his rheumatism, William Collins agreed to illustrate a new edition of Sir Walter Scott's *The Pirate* (1821), and Wilkie accompanied him on a trip to some of the settings in Scotland. Together, they rode through the countryside and took a steamship to the Shetland Islands, where Wilkie was amazed at the strength and directional sense of the ponies. Wilkie enjoyed the local hospitality, and travelling as his father's mature companion set the stage for later such sojourns with male friends. His retelling of an encounter with drunken Dutch sailors is one of the few times Wilkie lets a playful voice peek through in his memoirs of his father. Since William could not request permission to paint the sailors' boat in Dutch, he vainly tried to communicate by 'speaking English with as strong a Dutch accent as he could assume impromptu' (Part IV, Ch II). As had the Collinses' previous travels in Italy, the adventure made a deep impression on Wilkie, who was now eighteen years of age. Armadale, the name of a coastal town he and William visited, twenty years later became the title of one of Wilkie's novels.

By the time he was a young man, Willie had settled permanently on his middle name, Wilkie, as his primary name. Everyone in his life – friends, relatives, lovers, business associates, children of friends – called him Wilkie, and it was the appellation that would mark his gravestone. The first published piece that was thought to have carried his name, appearing as W. Wilkie Collins, was 'The Last Stage Coachman', printed with sketches in *The Illuminated Magazine* in August of 1843. Recently, Daniel Hack of the University of Michigan discovered an earlier signed piece: 'Volpurno – or the Student'. Published in New York's *The*

Albion on 8th July 1843 and shortly thereafter in other American periodicals, the story likely appeared earlier in an as yet untraced British publication. On 2nd January 2009, *The Times Literary Supplement* published 'Volpurno' in its entirety, properly attributed to Wilkie Collins for the first time in over 150 years.

Both 'Volpurno' and 'The Last Stage Coachman' are related by individuals who meet with solitary mysterious figures. 'Volpurno' is set in Venice, where a traveller encounters a grieving woman on the island of Lido. His guide recounts the events of her past, which form a sad tale of romance ruined by lunacy. The unnamed woman falls in love with a young astronomy student who marries her even though his youthful delusions of being haunted by an ugly woman phantom return as their nuptials approach. During the wedding day celebration, he goes completely mad, sprinting through the party with a bared sword in hopes of slaying the woman who haunts him. He jumps out of a window and runs across the countryside until he faints, to be nursed by his bride. Three days later, he expires at midnight, 'his favourite hour'. Never do we learn the identity of the ugly ghost haunting the student, why the prospect of his marriage brings her back, or why the actual wedding triggers a fatal relapse. The afflicted woman's death at the end of the traveller's visit relieves her suffering but does nothing to quiet the anxieties provoked by the spectre of madness that the story itself raises.

Haunting in a more literal manner is 'The Last Stage Coachman', a short piece exemplifying mid-Victorian fears about the consequences of technological progress. Sitting in a deserted inn yard, the narrator worries about servants who have lost their posts and stable boys made obsolete by the railway. Having pined for the coachman's 'unimpeachable top boots' and lamented the replacement of the coachman's cigar smoke with the steam of an engine, the speaker is suddenly joined by the corpse-like and bitter 'last' coachman. Nostalgia quickly turns into a grisly Gothic vision of a phantom coach sporting a driver dressed in garments made from the skins of railway employees, and the tale leaves one unsettled about the forms the past may continue to take in the future. Collins' budding narrative skill is evident in these early pieces, as is his ability to impress readers with vividly drawn characters in a short span of time.

Publishing under his own name and anonymously in increasingly visible venues, Wilkie still could not support himself financially. Dependent upon his parents, he began living an adult life that included vices of which they disapproved. The grown-up Wilkie, of moderate height at five feet six inches, had small, thin lips and grey eyes over which he always wore spectacles to correct extreme near-sightedness. His small stature and studious look were by no means a reflection of a reserved or bookish personality. Even though Wilkie's parents, and particularly his father, did not condone his indulgent habits, he shared accounts of his exploits with his mother. A few days after his twentieth birthday, he wrote to Harriet telling her of having been out on the town and drunk until dawn with his brother. Charley was growing into a more dashing young man. With blue eyes, flaming red hair, and a tall frame, Charley was quick to turn heads, but he was less attracted to the type of revelry that his older brother enjoyed. He had begun attending the Royal Academy Schools at age fifteen, where he behaved well, excelled in his studies and followed the religious examples set by his parents. He was more pained than pleased by Wilkie's aforementioned raucous birthday celebration. Having returned home after 4 a.m., Wilkie writes to Harriet on 13th January 1844, 'Charlie [sic] was so horrified at hearing the cock crow that he showed a disposition to whimper and said that people out so late as we, were not in a fit state to die.'

The careers of the differently disposed Collins brothers were ascendant, but their father's health was slowly deteriorating. In the spring of 1844, William developed a 'constant wearing cough', and by autumn, he exhibited the ominous symptom of coughing up blood (Part IV, Ch II). Through the ups and downs of his failing health, he travelled in search of better air to aid in his improvement, but the decline persisted. Harriet nursed him well, and the couple continued to encourage their sons' varied artistic pursuits as they grew into young adults.

Roaming and Writing

In August of 1844, Wilkie Collins travelled to mainland Europe for the first time without his family. Preparing for the trip, he was in high spirits and rather high strung. In a letter to his mother, Wilkie rants about proper travel gear because she has offered him the use of a carpet bag:

> … if there is nothing else for me, I suppose I must take it though I hate Carpet Bags with a great and bitter hatred. They don't protect you from damp, your brushes from breaking and your waistcoats from crumpling as a Portmanteau does. People sit upon a Carpet Bag because it is soft. Trunks tumble upon it for the same reason… It is the most disagreeable machine to pack – the most troublesome to unpack – the most impracticable to carry that human science ever invented…

> – 8th August 1844

Happily, by the end of the letter, Collins is able to report that he will borrow a less provoking case from Charles Ward, his fellow traveller. Charles and Wilkie met through their fathers, who were also friends. Although Charles would earn his living in banking, he and Wilkie shared a liking for art, which Charles had studied in Italy when the Collinses were residing there. The two formed a lasting friendship, and this early voyage took them to the Louvre (repeatedly), the famous Paris Morgue, and

Versailles. Charles would marry Wilkie's cousin Jane Carpenter within six months, but for the twenty-year-old Wilkie, this trip to Paris kicked off a time of guiltless pleasure as a bachelor.

The men frequented various theatres, gardens and cafes, worrying not at all about the social proprieties that so concerned Wilkie's father. Wilkie liked to wear flashy clothes, and Paris became a favourite place to shop for fine boots, which he always had trouble finding in a small enough size for his diminutive feet. A receded hairline emphasised his large and bulging forehead, and his head and shoulders continued to appear large in comparison to the rest of his body, but these traits did not hinder his ability to get on well with the ladies. To his mother, he unabashedly boasted of 'dissipating fearfully' (4th September 1844). He also enjoyed more chaste entertainments at concert or opera halls and was always pleased to find a good performance of Mozart. Ward and Collins enjoyed one another's company so much that they visited Europe together for the next four summers, even when Ward was hesitant to leave his new family.

Returning to England, Wilkie hardly threw himself into his work at Antrobus & Co. Instead, he wrote his first novel, *Ioláni*, for which neither he nor his father could ever find a publisher. The manuscript of *Ioláni* was lost from public view for nearly a century and a half before it surfaced in 1991, when it was sold to a private collector in New York City. The republication of this novel has provided a fresh and amusing look into Collins' early writing.

It is often tempting to look for the metaphorical 'seeds' of later greatness in an artist's early work, but one may also regard first novels as places where writers get inferior writing out of their creative systems. *Ioláni* can accommodate both approaches. The title character is an evil priest who not only impregnates then abandons Idía after a secret love affair, but also continues to threaten her and her adopted daughter Aimáta with violence and rape. In what Collins subtitled 'A Romance', one can spot concerns about victimised women, powerless children, and the institution of marriage that reappear throughout his career. The context for these themes, however, and Collins' portrayals of bloody Tahitian ceremonies so clearly belong to a long history of exoticising Pacific Islanders that it seems reductive to compare such scenes to the more sophisticated treatment of women and marriage in a later novel like *No Name*. At the same time, there are flashes of the type of psychological insight that mark some of the best moments of Collins' more mature fiction. He poignantly presents, for instance, the paradox of traumatic memory as it affects the wicked priest: 'It was a memory unlike other memories. It seized the attention and fascinated and wearied it at the same time. It became a still, slow, familiar torment, at once – a misery, whose stubborn vitality, nothing could injure or destroy' (Bk II, Ch IV). We also see Collins testing sensual boundaries with descriptions of the young Aimáta's adolescent body: 'In her restless slumber, her light clothing had become so discomposed, as to leave the upper part of her form – so delicate in shape, so enchantingly soft and dusky in hue – almost entirely uncovered. Her long hair, drooped over and partially concealed her neck and bosom' (Bk I, Ch III). Collins always enjoyed talking about women's bodies, but this level of scandalous detail he seems quickly to have realised would not be tolerated by the mainstream press.

On the whole, *Ioláni*'s powerful moments are eclipsed by cumbersome writing and plot devices verging on the absurd. When Ioláni escapes from exile and returns to Tahiti, for instance, his co-conspirator, a feared sorcerer, leaves him a cryptic symbolic trail. Of all things, the sorcerer chooses to communicate via plantain fruit. Ioláni discerns that the plantains 'seemed full of instruction', yet still manages to misunderstand their meaning of warning. Collins and his father initially blamed prudery for Victorian publishers' unwillingness to accept the novel, but more probably they rejected *Ioláni* on the grounds that it was a pretty bad book. Reportedly, even Collins laughed at its inferiority years later when he met a man who had evaluated the manuscript for one of the publishing houses.

In September of 1845, Collins returned to Paris by himself. Already a strong speaker of French and Italian, his fluency increased with each visit, and he had no wish to end his stay. After a few weeks, he had run out of money, and his parents were loath to continue funding such extravagant habits. He begged them to send more money, but at last he had to return to the dull post at the tea merchant's, which he held for only about six more months. Collins had no desire to settle down, but he lacked a way to support his desired lifestyle. What he needed was a profession, but what he wanted was to romp around Paris. To his father's disappointment, if not surprise, life as a clergyman had no appeal to Wilkie. Finally, William paid the fees for his eldest son to enter Lincoln's Inn as a student of law. Wilkie was somewhat interested in the law, but intense studying did not suit his temperament. Instead, he enjoyed dining with friends in London and imagining life in Rome as he continued writing his second novel, *Antonina*.

The book was unfinished on 17th February 1847, when William Collins died, and it remained incomplete while Wilkie handled the loss of his father. The death, after so many years of ailments and suffering, was not a shock to the family, and William was happy to have painted for as long as he possibly could. Sedated at the end with opium and surrounded by his family, William Collins exited the world with little commotion. Wilkie immediately abandoned his work in progress in order to fulfil William's expectations that his eldest son would pen his biography. An effective way to work through grief while honouring a loved one, writing the biography was a swift process. By late July, Collins was able to incorporate *Antonina* back into his writing schedule, and in August, he once again ventured to France with Charles Ward.

Wilkie relied on Harriet to finance his reluctant return voyage after Ward left, but much more intrigue was soon to be had back in England from Charles' younger brother Edward (Ned). The story of Collins' involvement in Ward's marriage is particularly interesting given its points of similarity to some of Collins' later plots. Ned Ward, in his early thirties, fell in love with a fourteen-year-old girl, Henrietta Ward (the families were not related), and Wilkie helped to arrange and execute their secret marriage to subvert her parents' objections. The stakes were high because Henrietta was not yet sixteen, and Ned could have faced jail time on kidnapping charges if she did not return to her parents' household after the secret marriage. The clandestine ceremony went off without a hitch; in turn, Collins was made godfather of the Wards' children and remained close to the family for the rest of his life.

Twenty-four years of age and not at all anxious to marry, Wilkie still resided with his mother and Charley. They all moved house in the summer of 1848 to 38 Blandford Square in the neigh-bourhood of Collins' birth, which he would forever favour. The house was full of merriment, and Collins' career was taking off. In November, *Memoirs of the Life of William Collins, Esq., R.A.* was published. In the tradition of biography at the time, Collins remained focused on his father's artistic identity as discrete from his identity as a husband and father. Accordingly, throughout the *Memoirs*, and quite conspicuously in the account of the Italian travels, Collins recounts his father's movements as if he had been travelling alone. He includes letters to Harriet that mention the boys but avoids discussing activities the family did together. *Memoirs* appropriately contains detailed descriptions of William Collins' paintings and also valuable primary source material in the form of extracts from his diary. Two volumes in length and dedicated to his father's patron Sir Robert Peel, Wilkie's first published book was a success. Several periodicals, including *Blackwood's* and *The Westminster Review*, gave it positive reviews, and Harriet was no doubt gratified with having financed her son's first foray into the book market.

In their new residence, Wilkie remained artistically stimulated on multiple fronts. The Collins family began to produce amateur theatricals with Wilkie producing as well as acting in plays such as Richard Sheridan's *The Rivals* (1775), an excellent comedy of doubled identities and satirical stabs at the conventions of genteel romance. In addition to writing, producing, and acting, Wilkie dabbled in painting. One time only, in 1849, a painting of Wilkie's was selected for the Royal Academy Exhibition (he would light-heartedly disparage the quality of *The Smuggler's Retreat* in later years). Also in 1849, Collins succeeded for the first time in persuading a publisher to print one of his novels. Bentley's, a most respectable publishing house, released *Antonina* in February of 1850.

A historical romance set in fifth-century Rome, *Antonina* required substantial amounts of research, which Collins carefully documented and presented in the novel's original annotations. Religious fanaticism, Christian and pagan, is Collins' target as he tells the story of the title character. Antonina, kept in isolation by her father to ensure her spiritual purity, is innocent of the accusations of vice that cause her father to drive her from home, but she does secretly love Hermanric, one of the Goth warriors blockading Rome. Hermanric's sister Goisvintha has sworn to avenge the deaths of her husband and children upon all Romans, especially those like Antonina, whose innocence matches that of her dead children. Goisvintha's vengeance leads to Hermanric's death, sending Antonina back to her now repentant father.

The novel delineates the bloody horrors that accompany war and pagan sacrifice, and its most memorable scene is a 'feast of Death' in which Vetranio, a decadent senator, urges his peers to die in an excess of wine presided over by a hideous corpse rather than perish in pathetic famine. In this scene at least, Collins' descriptive powers are admirable. In many others, his comparisons of ancient to modern Italy illustrate his familiarity with the country. The Pincian Hill, close to the Collinses' former abode and where the boys had spent much of their leisure time, serves as the novel's central locale. Chapter V begins with the narrator asking: 'Who that has been at Rome does not remember with delight the attractions of the Pincian Hill? Who, after toiling through the wonders of the dark, melancholy city, has not been revived by a visit to its shady walks, and by breathing its fragrant breezes?' Writing the novel not only provided Collins with an escape from his legal studies but also stoked his nostalgia, perhaps increased by the loss of his father, for a beloved place of his youth.

Biographical connections aside, *Antonina* is the novel one would be least likely to identify as belonging to Collins without prior knowledge of his authorship. Excepting small bits of effective satire, Collins includes little humour and writes in a heavy prose. The narrator tries the reader's patience with regular and elaborately justified digressions of the following sort: 'It is, however, necessary that the sphere in which the personages of our story are about to act should be in some measure indicated, in order to facilitate the comprehension of their respective movements' (Ch III). It is little wonder that Dorothy Sayers, who fully appreciated Collins' detective fiction and acknowledged its strong influence upon her own, saw nothing of value in *Antonina*. Most of its contemporary reviewers, though, were satisfied, finding the book impressive in historical accuracy and, as *The Athenaeum* put it, 'busy with life' (16th March 1850). By May, Bentley's was already issuing a second edition.

In the summer of 1850, Wilkie set out on a holiday adventure that would form the basis of his next published work, *Rambles Beyond Railways*. In these expeditions, he was accompanied by Henry Brandling, a young artist and friend. Hiking through Cornwall, climbing rocks, and crawling into mines, Collins was his most athletic and adventurous self during this trip. He remained away even when his mother unexpectedly decided to move house again, and his enthusiasm comes through in the illustrated travel narrative he promptly wrote in the months following the trip. Introducing the book to readers, Collins instructs, 'Toss him about anywhere, from hand to hand, as good-naturedly as you can; stuff him into your pocket when you get into the railway;

take him to bed with you, and poke him under the pillow.' *Rambles Beyond Railways* maintains this lively tone as Collins revels in escaping from the speed of modern transportation, exhorting readers to do the same. He delights in the discovery of the countryside on foot, far away from the commotion of city life and burdened only with a knapsack.

With an energy that transports readers, the book's chapters tell of fishing towns, boat races suddenly rained upon at Looe, a prison-like inn at Liskeard and a thrilling tour of the Botallack mine. Chapter X offers advice directly to those who might search for Land's End, 'Old horses startle you, scrambling into perilous situations, to pick dainty bits by the hill side; sheep, fettered by the fore and hind leg, hobble away desperately as you advance. Suddenly, you discern a small strip of beach shut in snugly between protecting rocks.' After a couple of chapters with surprisingly detailed portraits of Cornish theatre, the book concludes with intriguing stories of women's relationships that lie in stark contrast to the image of the two men actively traversing the Cornish coast. Collins' depiction of the Carmelite nuns at the village of Mawgan, who are never viewed by the public or even by their own servants, is respectful of their devotion and charitable works, but still he characterises their seclusion as a 'dreary life-in-death existence' that commences with a 'fatal ceremony'. The next tale is a legend about a pair of inseparable women who live humbly in a cottage. Their secluded companionship is so odd that the locals decide their existence must be supernatural and diabolical. After one of them dies, the other silently weeps herself to death at the bedside of the corpse.

Reaching the end of *Rambles Beyond Railways*, one realises that Collins' storytelling talents have progressed impressively. Never does the text read like a travelogue of lists or uncareful clichés. Rather, readers are apt to wish that the pair of travellers had experienced more adventures worthy of narration. First published on 20th January 1851 with Brandling's beautiful tinted lithographs, the book sold well enough to merit a second edition just a year later, which was especially advantageous for Collins because the contract entitled him to a share of the profits. His friendship with Brandling had turned out to be beneficial, but another friendship during this period would lead to the most significant professional partnership of Collins' life.

Since Wilkie's boyhood, Augustus Egg had been a friend of the Collins family. Pursuing an occupation that differed greatly from his father's gun-making, Egg was a painter known in the nineteenth century for his renditions of famous historical and literary scenes. With a substantial inheritance and secure income, Egg did not have to worry about selling his own paintings, so he acted as something of a patron to other artists. Egg also liked live performance and theatre, which is why he began acting alongside Charles Dickens in amateur theatricals. Although Egg was less extroverted and more modest in temperament than either Dickens or Collins, he did not hesitate to perform on the stage. Through Egg, Charles Dickens invited Wilkie to take part in an amateur production of Edward Bulwer-Lytton's *Not So Bad as We Seem* that was to benefit the Guild of Literature and Art. Collins played the valet of Dickens' character – a role that has been used to frame debates that persist to this day about the power dynamics between these two major novelists.

When they met on 12th March 1851, Dickens was thirty-nine years of age, and Collins was twenty-seven. The twelve-year age difference was enough to substantially distinguish the epochs of their boyhoods; Dickens came of age before the Regency was a distant cultural memory while Collins was a young man at the beginning of Victoria's reign. Nevertheless, the two men were fast friends. They shared an energetic disposition, a passion for detail, a taste for extravagant dress and a creative spark. Both men were also drawn to what others regarded as the seedy underside of Victorian life. Dickens had a lifelong habit of walking for miles, often through the streets of rough neighbourhoods, and Collins now joined him in regular jaunts through pub- and prostitute-lined streets. Prompting jealousy and disapprobation from Dickens' close friend and adviser, John Forster, who spitefully ignored the Collins / Dickens friendship in his *Life of Dickens* (1874), Dickens favoured carousing with Collins above staying at home with his nine young children and wife of nearly fifteen years.

To be befriended by Charles Dickens in the early 1850s was to receive the attention of a national, and increasingly international, celebrity. The scale of Dickens' fame was enormous, and the glow of his celebrity was no doubt part of the reason Collins was keen to be welcomed in his circle. The audience for *Not So Bad as We Seem* on 16th May 1851 included William Collins' former patron, Prince Albert, as well as Queen Victoria. Charley and Harriet Collins must have felt that their family's status was securely ascendant as they watched Wilkie perform in Dickens' show. Harriet was not unfamiliar with Dickens – he had commissioned a painting from William Collins in 1839 – but the friendship between her son and the great novelist would move far beyond that of artist and patron. In 1850, with the stated purpose of making himself even more of a household name, Dickens had launched a new venture: his own journal. *Household Words*, published weekly, immediately found the large readership for which Dickens hoped, and it became an important vehicle for Collins' work. The friendship was professional as well as personal, leading to joint literary endeavours and shared acquaintances. Through Dickens' assistant editor, W.H. Wills, Wilkie met Nina Chambers, who became one of his most intimate friends; in 1852 she married Frederick Lehmann, whose company Collins also esteemed. Nina was a woman whose intellectual engagement stimulated Collins, and he wrote long, engaging letters to both of the Lehmanns throughout his life. Along with close friends like the Wards, they functioned as extended family. Wilkie also grew close to Frances Dickinson, a woman using a male pseudonym whose writings he helped to publish and whose messy divorces provided Collins with firsthand accounts of the dangers of marriage laws.

In addition to rehearsals, the summer debut performance, and an autumn tour of *Not So Bad as We Seem*, journalistic writing busied Collins in 1851 and '52 and constituted a significant source of income. Perhaps the short length of the pieces was most accommodating of his late night tendencies. On 21st November 1851, being called to the Bar was primarily an occasion to drink. The next day, Wilkie wrote, 'I carried away much clarets and am rather a seedy barrister this morning. I think it must have been the <u>oaths</u> that disagreed with me.' Collins never wished or attempted to practise law, only ever calling himself a barrister to create a false identity. Through his twenties, Wilkie candidly indulged in his fondest pleasures. After night-time adventures, he did not hesitate to write letters to friends while drunk, openly describing his 'Bacchanalian state' then the following morning's roaring hangover (19th February 1852).

In late 1851, Collins also tried his hand at a Christmas Book, *Mr Wray's Cash Box*, which appeared on 13th December and received mixed reviews. Although it did not sell particularly well compared to Dickens' phenomenally popular Christmas works, the publishers moved enough copies to issue a second edition in 1852 (which is the date that, somewhat confusingly, appears on the title pages of even the first edition). Some reviewers, including John Ruskin, disparaged the work as weak Dickensian mimicry, but its worst fault, as Collins realised, was that his preface spoiled the suspense upon which the story depends. Knowing not only that the cash box contains a Shakespeare mask, but also how it came to contain the mask, leaves little of interest in the rest of the tale, and Collins was infuriated that Bentley's did not follow his instructions to delete the preface before printing. The incident did not stop him from writing justificatory prefaces for the rest of his career, about which his reviewers and peers consistently complained. An often overlooked aspect of this early book figures centrally in many of Collins' later novels and stories: post-traumatic short-term memory loss in which the afflicted person can recall events preceding the moment of trauma but not the trauma itself. Mr Wray's nerves, shaken most profoundly by the shattering of his precious Shakespeare mask, only remain steadied as long as his family and friends pretend that the robbery and the breaking of the mask all happened in a dream. Having replaced the mask, the family can easily maintain the conceit that the doctor claims is crucial to Mr Wray's survival.

Collins' early fascination with the workings of the human mind is also evident in a series of pieces on hypnotism and clairvoyance that he wrote for *The Leader*, a radical newspaper. 'Magnetic Evenings at Home' served as the title of six signed letters Collins published to argue for the legitimacy of clairvoyance and mesmerism. The letters, which appeared from January to April of 1852, were addressed to George Henry Lewes, one of the journal's founders. Collins' experiences at private gatherings in Somerset focused on 'extraordinary experiments' in 'Animal Magnetism' had convinced him of the power of mesmeric or hypnotic states. He further witnessed telepathic incidents involving the use of a polished coal mirror that, even accounting for the influence of hypnotism, seemed supernatural. A practitioner with 'petrifying power' strong enough to freeze a woman in the midst of dancing a polka especially impressed him. Lewes' response and Collins' subsequent retort show, not surprisingly, that the respectful disagreement between the advocate and the sceptic never abated. Collins' other significant interchange with *The Leader* concerned his objection to the editorial practice of permitting a writer's personal religious beliefs or doubts to appear in one's writing about politics or current events. Unable to find common ground on the subject with Edward Pigott, the journal's controlling proprietor whom Collins continued to regard as a friend, Collins insisted that any future pieces he wrote for *The Leader*, which included several reviews of theatrical productions, books and art exhibits, appear unsigned.

Collins' first two pieces for *Household Words* were both concerned with slightly different subjects: murder and France. 'A Terribly Strange Bed' (24th April 1852) tells of a Paris gambling house whose thieving owners use a lethal contraption to noise-lessly lower a bed's canopy upon unsuspecting (and drugged) sleepers. Once they have taken the victim's winnings, the thieves dispose of the suffocated bodies with suicide notes attached. One sees a flash of Collins' ability to write suspense when the narrator has discovered the device and must figure out how to flee safely from a house full of people he knows are trying to kill him. A year later, Collins placed a longer, richer tale in the journal.

'Gabriel's Marriage' (16th–23rd April 1853) is set in Brittany during the Revolution. While dying, Gabriel's grandfather con-fesses to believing that his own son, Gabriel's father Paul, killed a man. The story poignantly presents the subsequent intensity and unsettling terror of a son suspecting that his father is a murderer. Gabriel ultimately discovers that the man his father assaults survived the attack to become a renowned priest performing illicit Catholic ceremonies on ships to escape the revolutionary violence. The tale is striking in its sympathetic portrayal of the Catholic priest and its moving description of the church at sea: 'Here was no artificial pomp, no gaudy pro-fusion of ornament, no attendant grandeur of man's creation. All around this church spread the hushed and awful majesty of the tranquil sea. The roof of this cathedral was the immeas-urable heaven, the pure moon its one great light, the countless glories of the stars its only adornment.' Collins' distaste for the trappings of organised religion is plain, and his positive presentation of the clandestine Catholic ceremony becomes a useful point of comparison for Catholic characters in some of his later works.

Prolific journalism in no way kept Collins away from the theatre. The successful production of *Not So Bad as We Seem* that had premiered in May of 1851 returned to the stage for a tour in May of 1852 with Wilkie in a more substantial role. The cast reassembled for a final set of performances in August and September, after which Collins joined the Dickens family for a long visit. This was Collins' first time residing in Dickens' household, and, while Dickens was working on the mammoth *Bleak House*, Collins was content to spend the same working hours completing *Basil*, the novel he had been working on intermittently since early in the year.

Basil begins with the provocative question, 'What am I now about to write?'. What Wilkie Collins did write was an early, shocking novel of sensation. The term, used pejoratively by most critics at the time, referred to fiction that was intentionally designed to jolt its readers, strongly affecting their nerves and sensations. Some of the most common features of the genre are concealed or bigamous marriages; hidden or lost letters; stolen, mistaken, or assumed identities; newly discovered 'blood' relatives; drug use and/or poisoning; spying; and strained coincidences. As with all literary forms, however, sensation fiction was by no means a discrete entity. It regularly overlapped with Gothic fiction, domestic romance, psychological realism, melodrama, and the development of detective fiction. In seeking to categorise a work as sensational, one looks for some combination of the elements above, an especially heavy dependence on strained coincidences, and settings where the most shocking of intrigues are discovered within familiar domestic spaces often belonging to the higher social classes. Most reviewers and scholars in the nineteenth and well into the twentieth century dismissed sensation fiction, even when well written, either as a silly waste of time or as a harmful habit akin to addiction that would fuel moral degeneration and vice in impressionable, and mostly women, readers. Increasingly, scholars in the latter decades of the twentieth century refocused critical attention on the ways in which these works fundamentally interrogate the way power is routed through social structures, such as marriage, and on the manner in which the shocking scenarios also raise deeper questions of human psychology, identity, and motivation. Collins' works fall in various positions on this spectrum and often demonstrate why categorisation is so difficult.

Reviews of *Basil* praised Collins' excellent writing while regretting its condemnable topic. The critiques sketch the grievances that would persistently trouble writers of sensation fiction: its atmosphere was 'vicious', its depictions of vice full of 'hateful details', and its message insufficiently edifying.[2] What was so offensive? *Basil* is disowned for falling in love at first sight – a device Collins would employ repeatedly – and secretly marrying Margaret Sherwin, the daughter of a linen-draper. On the night the married couple intend to expose their union and begin living together as husband and wife, Margaret flees with her father's clerk, Mannion. Basil follows them, eavesdrops on their triumphant reunion, then nearly kills Mannion, who turns out to be seeking revenge against Basil's father for an injustice done to his own father. Mannion survives in disfigured form only to torment Basil until the two quarrel and Mannion falls off a cliff.

More masterful than its plot is Collins' use of point of view to cast the novel's attempted murderer as its hero. Basil flies into a rage, attacking Mannion so brutally that Mannion's face is disfigured, yet the duped protagonist remains sympathetic. Murder was Basil's conscious intent, his 'ONE THOUGHT', but because Mannion chooses to personally punish rather than to formally prosecute his attacker, Basil emerges as the victim of a scheming villain instead of as the victim of his own folly (Part II, Ch VII). Collins' first non-historical novel, *Basil* also shows him struggling to develop women characters. Basil's sister Clara is angelically perfect, and Margaret is flightily shallow, but Mrs Sherwin is an effective early drawing of an emotionally battered wife. Also noteworthy, given Collins' later achievements in detective fiction and Dickens' Inspector Bucket in *Bleak House*, is Collins using a predilection for touring the streets with 'detective policemen' as evidence of Basil's older brother Fred's dissolution.

While Wilkie's storytelling talent grew steadily, his brother Charley was insecure about his art, physically weak, and susceptible to depression. His strict religious practices, such as fasting, did little to improve his health. Studying at the Royal Academy with contemporaries, Charley closely involved himself with the Pre-Raphaelite Brotherhood, a group of men who challenged dominant aesthetic tastes by emphasising naturalism and sensuality over what they viewed as the artificial formality of the artwork that institutions such as the Royal Academy chose to value. Not as secure in his artistic vision as many of his peers, the closest of whom were Holman Hunt and John Everett Millais, Charley was never admitted as an official Brother, which further weakened his confidence. Wilkie, as he expressed in an anonymous *Bentley's* review of the Summer Exhibition at the Royal Academy in 1851, was gently critical of the Pre-Raphaelite movement. He saw too much attention to detail at the cost of larger artistic vision. As much as Wilkie rejected his father's view of religion and conventional marriage mores, he did not reject the artistic tradition of which his father was so much a part and from which Charley diverged. Although Wilkie respectfully sat for Millais, whose excellent 1851 rendering of him at age twenty-seven hangs in London's National Portrait Gallery, he did not hesitate to poke fun at the vanity of aspiring artists in his next novel, *Hide and Seek*.

As Charley faced internal artistic struggles, it was a physical challenge that slowed Wilkie's work on *Hide and Seek*, which he began in April of 1853. This episode was probably his first battle with gout, an acutely painful form of arthritis, often hereditary, in which excess amounts of sodium urate inflame and cripple joints, especially in the feet and legs. The rheumatic affliction that pained his father, once present, would never fully exit Wilkie's life. In late June, he began to mend, telling Edward Pigott on the 25th, 'I am much better – but not strong enough yet to do more than "toddle" out for half an hour at a time with a stick,' and on 7th July, he told Harriet that he had 'begun the great reformation'. Once strong enough, Collins accepted an invitation to join Dickens in Boulogne, where he was on holiday with his family and Augustus Egg festively marking the end of the nearly two years he had spent writing *Bleak House*. Collins felt his spirits lift even as he continued to heal. He wrote to Charley on 12th August 1853, 'The weather is lovely – glorious sunshine and cool air. I go on very well, except my legs, which are not as strong yet as they ought to be.'

The trio had so much fun together that Dickens easily persuaded Collins and Egg to continue the revelry by accompanying him to Switzerland and Italy in the autumn. Leaving his large family, Dickens was excited to travel with two pleasurable bachelors, and they benefited from the extraordinary welcome Dickens enjoyed in each new city. The two-month journey commenced in early October 1853, as did a fierce moustache-growing contest. Dickens mocked the 'straggling, wandering, wiry, stubbly, formless' attempts of Collins and Egg in his letters home and unsuccessfully tried to force a concession of defeat by shaving his own beard, which he fancied would serve as 'a dread warning to competitors'.[3] The younger gentlemen persisted in their efforts, and although Dickens claimed victory, one has to wonder whether the prodigious beards Dickens and Collins sported in their later years might have been a continuation – articulated or otherwise – of the earlier showdown.

Wilkie's letters, which he hoped would form the basis of a published account of the trip, recorded various points of interest. He marvelled at the roads cut through the Alps and the region's natural beauty but was unsparing and harsh in his revulsion from the people who inhabited the Swiss valleys, emphasising birth defects in the population and their grotesquely large goitres. He movingly told Harriet about the 'very touching and solemn sight' of a fourteen-year-old girl's body embalmed for two hundred years alongside her father's corpse in the Church of St Thomas at Lausanne (16th October 1853). When the group reached Italy, Wilkie was overcome with emotion, for this was his first return visit since his residency there as a child. He wrote at length to Charley, updating him on Naples and explaining that Rome, especially the Pincian Hill, felt unchanged in comparison to the days when they were boys (13th November 1853). He also recorded a thrilling spotting of the Pope when he was separated from Dickens and Egg.

Collins was the baby of the group at age twenty-nine to Dickens' forty and Egg's thirty-seven, but already he seems to have been growing accustomed to poor health. Dickens described a Collins 'much troubled with a "tightness" in his inside' and complained that he was 'always reporting on its condition to us'.[4] Dickens' grumblings did not stop there. The men continued to enjoy each other's company, but their constant togetherness resulted in the kind of tension that tends to arise on long trips. Dickens liked to be in charge (one of his wife's early nicknames for him was 'Bully'), and he was used to others following his will. Possibly envious of Collins' more refined and 'gentlemanly' knowledge of painting, Dickens refrained from visiting artists' studios with Collins and Egg. He was increasingly bothered by what he characterised as Collins' constant lecturing about all things Italian, and Collins' familiarity with Italy would surely have lessened Dickens' role as tour guide and leader. Egg's mild disposition probably helped to diffuse the tension between the two stronger personalities, and his incompetence with other tongues provided hearty amusement. Dickens wrote, 'I cannot remember what Egg... called a Bird yesterday, in his second or third endeavour to explode a Substantive on a waiter. But it was something compounded of English and French with an Italian termination – something like Birdoisella.'[5] Unfortunately, we cannot supplement Dickens' account with Egg's own thoughts on his forays into Romance languages because his diary of the trip, if it survived, remains undiscovered.

The tone of Collins' letters remained unphased by Dickens' complaints, although he did remark upon Dickens' constant linguistic drilling of Egg. All three were harassed by a bad opera in Milan and travelling crowds, especially on the steamship *Valetta*, which they boarded during its stop at Genoa. The boarding agent permitted twice as many people to embark as there were beds on board, so the trio slept on the deck in the rain. The next night, Dickens was fortunate enough to secure a berth in a cabin (whose occupant evicted his own son) while Collins and Egg slept in the ship's store room with an old man, the steward, loads of provisions and a cat. They were all quite happy to reach Naples. Subsequently, Collins was awed by the artwork he saw in Venice. In a letter whose aesthetic appreciation would have made his father proud, Collins raved about Tintoretto's work in great detail and declared the Venetians 'the most <u>original</u> race of painters that the world has yet seen' (25th November 1853).

Unpredictable low moments and personal quirks aside, Collins, Dickens, and Egg enjoyed a wonderful trip, and none regretted what Collins called the 'luxurious, dandy-dillettante sort of life' of their travels (25th November 1853). In the two years since Egg had been the means of bringing Collins into Dickens' amateur play, the three had formed enduring friendships. They socialised at the Garrick Club with other men who patronised or participated in the literary and dramatic arts, and they reunited on stage in Dickens' theatrical productions. Wilkie continued travelling regularly, often with Dickens, but still had to monitor his finances to ensure that he could continue to fund the adventures he so enjoyed.

Sensational Developments

Returning from the Continent in time for Christmas in 1853, Collins resumed work on the novel he had paused before the trip. For the next several years, he worked impressively in various literary modes, writing short stories and novellas for several periodicals as he refined and expanded his narrative talent. Increasingly, he wrote collaboratively with Dickens in multiple genres, including drama. Collins also continued to travel as frequently as possible, often joining Dickens in France. He had planned to rebound financially from the extended 1853 journey abroad with a book chronicling the trip, but when Bentley's rejected the proposal, *Hide and Seek* promptly recalled his attention.

Critics have focused heavily on *Hide and Seek*'s few autobiographical parallels, such as the protagonist's distaste for working as a clerk at a tea merchant, but such an approach oversimplifies both the novel's plot and Collins' own life. Collins' claims in the preface that the novel has a basis in observed experience do not differ much from the truth claims of many novels (since the genre's beginnings) or from many of Collins' other works, including ones that feature adventures in India and Tahiti, places he never saw. Finished speedily and making its way into print by June of 1854, *Hide and Seek* follows *Basil* as another early example of sensation fiction, and its strained coincidences are many.

Valentine Blythe, a gently mocked artist, adopts a deaf and mute girl whose past he refuses to explain. Scandalous gossip persists about Mary (called 'Madonna') Grice's origins even though one would expect Mrs Blythe's devotion to the girl to lessen speculation that her birth resulted from an extramarital affair on Mr Blythe's part. In truth, a parental version of 'love at first sight' for the pretty child draws Blythe to her at a circus performance. A friend and student of Blythe, Zack Thorpe, sparks an intense crush from Madonna, then turns out to be her half-brother. The rebellious Zack also jumps into a bar brawl to aid a stranger who later reveals himself as Madonna's long lost uncle.

The story may not be as plausible as Collins insisted, but the novel's brisk pace and engaging characters are immediately intriguing. Madonna stands as an early example of Collins' considerate representation of characters with disabilities – characters most Victorian novelists ignored or portrayed as unsympathetic outcasts. Madonna, orphaned as a newborn, is cared for by the loving Mrs Peckover but still must work for an abusive circus manager. She loses her hearing after falling from a horse at the age of seven, and Collins' portrait of her subsequent muteness touchingly explains, 'she might as well be without a voice at all; for she has nothing but her memory left to tell her that she has one' (Bk I, Ch V). The accuracy of these sensory details comes from Collins' heavy borrowing from John Kitto's *The Lost Senses* (1845). Kitto, deaf himself, compiled narratives of deaf, mute, and blind people, and Collins continually drew from such source texts throughout his career.

Madonna's life also significantly suggests that biological bonds, while strong, are not the ones that ultimately determine kinship. After suckling the orphaned Madonna, Mrs Peckover simply becomes her mother, and wet nursing, which establishes a quasi-biological link through nourishment, is not the only way in which alternative family structures arise. When Mr Blythe offers to rescue the girl from the abusive circus master, both Mrs Peckover and Madonna are heartbroken at parting, but Madonna swiftly comes to love Blythe as an adopted father, accepting multiple sets of parental figures. Blythe also stands as a father figure for Zack Thorpe, whose antipathy for his unsympathetic biological father further cements the point. The family structures most intact at the novel's conclusion are decidedly not the ones that privilege blood relations.

Even when dealing with such serious matters, the book maintains a light tone with exceptional moments of humour. The character of Mat – comfortably rough in the skullcap he wears after an Indian scalping – provides an eccentric and refreshing contrast to the more refined artists. In an uproariously ironic moment, Zack kindly and genuinely warns the scalped man against giving Madonna a bracelet made of hair, then worries he has caused offence. Blythe also baffles Mat by gazing adoringly at Mat's biceps, begging for permission to paint the 'splendid muscular development' of the man's arms (Bk II, Ch X).

Hide and Seek received excellent reviews praising its style and tone. Collins wisely limited the time his publishers owned the copyright so that he would have more control over, and receive greater profits from, future editions. Revising the 1854 edition for publication in 1861, he tightened up the prose substantially and took the rare step of changing the ending to reunite more of the characters. Fortuitously, since Collins had dedicated the book to him, Dickens loved it, and the two had joint cause for celebration when Dickens came to London from France to deliver the final instalments of *Hard Times* in July of 1854. Planning the visit, Dickens made a strong case for Collins' companionship: 'The interval I propose to pass in a career of amiable dissipation and unbounded license in the metropolis. If you will come and breakfast with me about midnight—anywhere—any day—and go to bed no more until we fly to these pastoral retreats—I shall be delighted to have so vicious an associate.'[6] The sharing of implicitly sexual debauchery, plus whatever else constituted Dickens' notion of sleep-prohibitive 'unbounded license', evidently moved beyond Collins' routine drunkenness.

Collins then joined the entire Dickens family on their summer holiday in Boulogne, where the two 'vicious' associates recuperated for a long spell and even the workaholic Dickens allowed himself to relax until late September. The pair hoped to resume their less wholesome urban fun in February of 1855 when Dickens persuaded Collins to join him on a nine-day trip to Paris, but Wilkie fell very ill with what was probably a venereal disease. Whatever his ailment, the fact that he did not mention it in a letter to his mother on 14th February suggests that it was not of the ordinary variety. Several things distinguish this illness from Wilkie's inherited gout. For one thing, he was not consistently disabled by it. He was well enough to spend the late mornings and early afternoons reading and writing, and he even continued to go to the theatre in the evenings, which would have been painful in a rheumatic condition. What he avoided were alcohol and extended outings or walks – activities that would have taxed him if he was low on energy or if he had an uncomfortable skin condition. After returning to England, Collins remained unwell until the middle of April, and Dickens' letter to him on 4th March 1855 contains a metaphorically veiled reference to sexually transmitted disease. Offering a visit during which he will 'inspect the Hospital', Dickens writes, 'I am afraid this relaxing weather will tell a little faintly on your medicine, but I hope you will soon begin to see land beyond the Hunterian ocean.' John Hunter was the well-known and respected author of *Treatise on the Venereal Disease* (1786) who had injected himself with gonorrhea (and, accidentally, syphilis) as part of his medical research. The cover of an 1818 edition of Hunter's work showed two ships at sea, illuminating Dickens' meaning further. What with Wilkie and Charley still sharing the house at 17 Hanover Terrace with their mother, Harriet would of course have been aware of Collins' illness, but medical men could certainly have offered explanations to obscure venereal disease as the cause.

By May of 1855, Collins had recovered so completely that he took to the stage. He wrote *The Lighthouse*, and Dickens cast himself, his daughter Mary and sister-in-law Georgina Hogarth, Collins, Augustus Egg, and Mark Lemon in an amateur production that filled a theatre space in the Dickens home for three nights beginning on 16th June. Dickens wanted to keep the production secret so that its surprise debut would generate buzz, which helped lead to a July benefit performance in Kensington. No professional productions immediately followed, but the disappointment did not discourage Collins from future playwriting, either individually or collaboratively with Dickens.

Collins had also been writing more pieces for *Household Words*, which would turn out to be the venue for his most popular novels yet, as well as other journals. Splitting stories into four instalments served as practice for the later weekly serialisation of his longer novels. Two pieces from 1855, both set in Italy, show Collins engaging with Catholicism at multiple levels and in ways that reappear in his work several years later. 'The Yellow Mask' (*Household Words,* July 1855) shows Father Rocco heartlessly scheming to win back Church lands and riches by manipulating his niece Maddalena's marriage to the nobleman Fabio d'Ascoli. After devastating the hopes of Nanina, an impoverished girl whom d'Ascoli truly loves, Rocco interferes with d'Ascoli's second marriage when Maddalena dies. Nearly killing the young man with tactics combining Gothic and sensation plots, Rocco uses a sculpture of his dead niece to make a plaster mask of her face, which he convinces one of d'Ascoli's spurned lovers to wear at a ball. Thanks to the instincts of her plucky dog, Nanina discovers Rocco's trick, and its revelation restores d'Ascoli to health. Indeed, with growls that lead Nanina to a hidden spot from which she can eavesdrop on Rocco, Scarammuccia the poodle is a contender for the title of first canine detective, a designation that usually falls upon the Scottish terrier Tommie in Collins' 'My Lady's Money' (1877). The priest villain of 'The Yellow Mask' justifies his actions with the dangerous rhetoric of the institution he serves, but the story does not disparage individual belief in Catholicism. 'The Monktons of Wincot Abbey' depicts the Church in equally unappealing terms but focuses even more on the plight of a sympathetic Catholic individual.

Published in November and December of 1855, the subject of 'The Monktons of Wincot Abbey' was too disturbing for *Household Words,* so Collins placed it with *Fraser's Magazine.* Alfred Monkton, whose Catholic lineage is full of insane people, lives in seclusion for fear of having inherited the family madness. After his uncle dies in a duel, Alfred is haunted by the unburied body and convinced that the only way to escape a prophecy that 'Monkton's race shall pass away' is to discover his uncle's corpse and place it in the family tomb (Ch IV). Primarily through the aid of the unnamed narrator, Alfred learns the location of the corpse and arranges for the rotting body to be removed from a monastery's outbuilding for transport by sea. The monks appear a bit mad themselves (unsurprisingly, given the story's later title) and have refused to bury the gentleman because he died in a duel, a practice banned by the Pope. On their way back to England, with the corpse as secret cargo, the narrator and Monkton are betrayed by a Maltese boy whose revelation leads the crew to mutiny during a storm. After the coffin sinks into the sea, the devastated Alfred sinks into a fever, mercifully unable to remember the nautical trauma as he dies. Alfred's death extinguishes the Monkton bloodline, leaving the reader to question whether Monkton was actually mad or just prudent in following an accurate prophecy. The Gothic influences in this excellent story echo Collins' early published pieces, as does its deeper questioning of the origins of mental instability – a theme whose importance Collins emphasises in his revision of the story's title to 'Brother Griffith's Story of Mad Monkton' in *The Queen of Hearts* (1859).

The year of 1855 concluded on high notes for Wilkie. In November, he was thrilled to see that Émile D. Forgues published a sweeping and positive assessment of his early works in *La Revue des Deux Mondes.* French novelists, such as Balzac, had influenced Collins in his twenties, and Collins' challenging of accepted literary conventions as well as his critical view of English hypocrisy played well with French audiences. Collins followed some of Forgues' suggestions, credited the early endorsement with increasing his artistic confidence, and happily engaged Forgues to translate several of his later novels into French. Adding to his rising international reputation as a gifted storyteller, Collins published his first piece of non-fiction for *Household Words* in December with 'The Cruise of the Tomtit'. The playful autobiographical account of Collins and Edward Pigott, as Mr Jollins and Mr Migott, grew out of the pair's sailing trip in September. Pigott and Collins had been students together at Lincoln's Inn, where neither of them cared much about or passed their exams. The men remained friends even after their disputes over religion at *The Leader*. Pigott was an avid sailor, and their trip to the Scilly Isles with a crew of three entertaining brothers sold Collins permanently on the diversions of sailing, especially with Pigott's company.

The accumulation of so many short published pieces led Collins to compile a book collection early in 1856. Adding one new composition to five from *Household Words*, he called the book *After Dark* and used a frame concept to link the stories. For the frame story, some have suggested that Wilkie lifted heavily from his mother's diary, which was never published but which he was editing at the time as the two considered publishing a fictionalised version under Wilkie's name. It is interesting to examine Collins' correspondence on the subject of his mother's diary and his manner of dismissing its literary value, but the diary did not serve as a direct source text for *After Dark*. The collection's stories are fictionally penned by Leah Kerby, whose husband, a painter trying to stave off blindness, narrates them in the hopes of generating income while forced to rest his eyes. Although Leah Kerby and Harriet Collins are both married to artists, they occupy very different social positions, and the frame story does not replicate Harriet's actual diary. As Catherine Peters points out, it is far more productive to consider the influence of Harriet's diary on Wilkie's later novel *No Name* than to suggest that he plagiarised it for *After Dark*. The collection sold very well, and shortly after its publication in February of 1856, Collins joined Dickens in Paris. Arriving on the 27th, he was delighted with the cottage Dickens had procured, but for much of the six-week stay, Collins suffered from a painful attack of rheumatism all through his body.

Around this time, and definitely by the early 1860s, Collins began using laudanum as a component of his pain management regimen. Laudanum was an easily available mixture of opium dissolved in alcohol that was present in many realms of Victorian society. In small doses, mothers and nursemaids administered the solution – against increasingly forceful admonitions from medical men – to quiet fussy infants. Starving members of the labouring classes resorted to the inexpensive remedy of chewing opium to fend off hunger pains, effectively illustrated in Elizabeth Gaskell's *Mary Barton* (1848). Wilkie said that his mother's pragmatic attitude towards Samuel Taylor Coleridge's addiction to opium made a lasting impression on him, and Wilkie's own father used laudanum to relieve symptoms at the end of his life. Opium use was not a recreational drug habit for Collins or a vice. Rather, it was a pain remedy that ultimately came with the high price of addiction.

When Collins was ill in Paris, Dickens was sympathetic, and when Collins was well, the two continued to enjoy daily outings and to attend theatres. Wilkie also had to make time to work on *A Rogue's Life*, which appeared in *Household Words* from 1st to 29th March 1856 and whose instalments he was composing close to each printing deadline. The novella's spirited rogue, Dr Frank Softly, is as serious about doctoring as Collins was about lawyering. Softly refuses to be industrious about anything but irresponsibility and supports himself with everything from secretarial work at a literary society to counterfeit portrait making. Collins' presentation of less-than-scrupulous art dealers is indebted to his grandfather's *Memoirs of a Picture* (1805), a disjointed, schizophrenic and sprawling three-volume work that nonetheless influenced Wilkie. The rogue's life finds focus when he falls in love at first sight with the mysterious Dr Dulcifer's daughter Alicia, and his romantic pursuit leads him unwillingly into another counterfeiting operation: the felonious forging of coins. After a Scottish marriage by declaration and subsequent capture by a persistent Bow Street runner, the rogue is transported to Australia, where Alicia joins him using the alias of a widow. Employed as Alicia's servant until he has earned enough privileges to move in more elevated social circles, the rogue hardly suffers; for his own wife 'made a very indulgent mistress' ('Postscript').

While Wilkie was imagining and sometimes pursuing the life of a rogue abroad, Charley lived a more settled life with Harriet, saving one possible incident that sounds more characteristic of his older brother's usual behaviour than his own. In the summer of 1856, Charley was rumoured to have taken up with a woman his friends regarded as undesirable. Details are scant, and Wilkie does not mention the relationship or make any clear allusions to it in his surviving letters to Harriet. Writing from Paris on 19th August, he includes instructions for some manuscript pages that he thinks will be delivered to the publisher more swiftly 'if Charley is at home' when they arrive, and on 1st September, when Harriet was on a pleasant visit to Maidenhead, Wilkie wrote, 'I am glad Charley is with you.' Such general statements in isolation do not suggest much, but they may bolster the strong case that Catherine Peters makes for Charley Collins as the unnamed and longtime friend whom John Everett Millais describes in a letter to Holman Hunt. Millais worried that this friend had formed a 'disreputable kind of secret connection' and urged Hunt to help him remove the woman from their friend's confidence.[7]

After a summer of more sailing with Pigott and another holiday in Boulogne with the Dickens family, Collins joined the permanent staff of *Household Words* in October of 1856. It was

Dickens who initiated the negotiations that led Collins to become a staff member. Like many contributors, Collins was not always comfortable with the anonymity accompanying publication in *Household Words*. The journal, 'Conducted by Charles Dickens', shared the practice of many others by insisting that individual authors sacrifice bylines in order to create a consistent collective voice for the periodical. Collins agreed to *Household Words*' practice of removing his name from shorter pieces, but he was not to become a writer whose identity Dickens completely erased. It was Collins' condition upon joining the staff that his next novel be published in the journal with his own name attached. Although Dickens doubted that Collins' novels would be as profitable as his shorter works, he consented to give Collins the byline and ultimately was proven wrong about the value of Collins' work. Collecting a fixed salary of five guineas per week, Collins' income steadied itself.

Some of Collins' best work for *Household Words* appeared in the special Christmas issues, called numbers, that were always collaborative ventures. The first ones were unrelated stories about Christmas itself, but in 1852, Dickens began to yoke the stories together around a frame concept, and the stories had little if anything to do with Christmas. The title of the 1854 number, *The Seven Poor Travellers*, presents its unifying theme, and Collins' solicited contribution was the fourth traveller's tale. A story of blackmail and romance, it was subsequently reprinted as 'The Lawyer's Story of A Stolen Letter' in *After Dark* (1856) and has the distinction of being regarded as the first British detective story. Many critics have noted its similarity to Edgar Allan Poe's 'The Purloined Letter' (1845), and Poe's stories were important influences as Collins developed longer mystery narratives. Their literary circles also overlapped: Poe had reviewed Dickens' *Barnaby Rudge* (1841), which prominently features a raven, before penning his famous poem bearing that bird's name. Following the 1854 Christmas number, Collins' tales would appear in the special issues for the next seven years, and he was the only author with whom Dickens ever collaborated on the frame stories themselves.

In *The Wreck of the Golden Mary* (1856), Dickens begins the number in the voice of Captain Ravender, but after the ship sinks on its way to California, Collins takes over the narration in the voice of first mate, John Steadiman. In between, five other writers' tales keep the castaways calm in an attempt to distract their minds from cannibalism. It is a lively collection of stories, and critics continue to debate the degree to which Collins and Dickens narratively enact a power struggle that may have been present in their friendship. Whether one views Collins, in the voice of Steadiman, pushing against, subverting, or submitting to Dickens' authority, his narrative voice has the last word in the number, and the men's joint literary endeavours only increased. Since Collins generally disliked the Christmas holiday, calling the day 'horrid' in a letter of 28th December 1885, it is ironic that some of his most successful collaborations with Dickens, who loved the holiday, stemmed from the Christmas numbers and Dickens' elaborate Twelfth Night festivities. For the 1856–7 season, they worked together on a stage play, *The Frozen Deep*, in addition to the Christmas number.

The Frozen Deep was inspired by the impassioned debate following the failed 1845 Franklin Expedition in which Sir John Franklin sought to discover the Northwest Passage. Dr John Rae's report of evidence that the last surviving members of the crew had resorted to cannibalising the corpses of their peers in a futile attempt at survival outraged Dickens and many others. It would certainly have been understandable for Dickens and others to imagine cannibalism as an honourable act following the noble death of comrades in such circumstances. *The Frozen Deep*, however, showcases a very different view of self-sacrifice. Richard Wardour, hopelessly in love with Clara Burnham, bitterly vows revenge upon the man whose marriage proposal Clara accepts. Distracting himself by joining an Arctic expedition that becomes stranded two years later, Wardour realises that another crewman,

Frank Aldersley, is Clara's fiancé. When Wardour and Aldersley leave the others in search of help, Wardour valiantly battles his desire to kill his rival, ultimately saving Aldersley's life to ensure Clara's future happiness. Pursuing a fairly unusual remedy for domestic boredom and anxiety, the women in the story have headed to the Arctic to alleviate their concerns about the men. Their extraordinary arrival enables the moving melodramatic tableau of the closing scene: on the ice, Clara cradles in her arms the dying Wardour, whose final words plead, 'Kiss me, sister, kiss me before I die!'.

Collins and Dickens had begun discussing the plot in Paris in the spring of 1856 while Collins was also beginning a new novel, and in August, they worked on the play together for a few more weeks in France. Spanning several months, the collaboration was multifaceted. After Dickens articulated the original idea, the two conversed about it and developed a story that also included Collins' ideas; Collins was responsible for writing a script that Dickens revised in consultation with him; the two corresponded regularly via letter not only about dialogue revisions but also about Dickens' handling of the staging; and they split the leading male roles. The playbill presents Tavistock House Theatre 'Under the Management of Charles Dickens' and calls *The Frozen Deep* a 'Romantic Drama, in Three Acts, by Mr Wilkie Collins'. Here, then, Dickens' public advertisement of the men's joint work emphasises individual responsibilities in marked contrast to his presentation of the Christmas numbers and to the collaborative spirit that permeated the production. Dickens was at the helm, but he consistently respected Collins as a more experienced playwright and consulted him even about staging details. On 1st November 1856, after receiving some feedback from John Forster, Dickens wrote,

Stanfield wants to cancel the chair altogether, and to substitute a piece of rock on the ground, composing with the Cavern. That, I take it, is clearly an improvement. He has a happy idea of

painting the ship which is to take them back, ready for sailing, on
the sea... Will you dine with us at 5 on Monday before Rehearsal.
We can then talk over Forster's points?

The discourse indicated in these letters demonstrates that Dickens
was reluctant to impose his own artistic vision upon Collins' without respectful discussion. Another letter requests, 'I should like
to shew [*sic*] you some cuts I have made in the second act (subject
to Authorial sanction of course). They are mostly verbal, and all
bring the Play closer together' (9th October 1856).

The completed version of the script worked well in performance as Collins took the role of Aldersley and Dickens played
Wardour. Several friends, including Augustus Egg and Edward
Pigott, as well as Dickens' relatives, constituted the rest of the
cast. The show garnered excellent reviews, especially of Dickens'
tear-jerking enactment of the final scene. Queen Victoria commissioned a private performance on 4th July, after which she sent
enthusiastic compliments to Collins. Though Dickens and Collins
had worked together often, *The Frozen Deep* was their closest collaboration yet, and one spots creative cross-fertilisation in other
works they published individually during this period. Various
combinations of self-sacrifice (particularly in the name of romantic love), doubled identities, and the French Revolution appear
in several of their works, including Collins' stories 'The Lady
of Glenwith Grange' (1856 in *After Dark*) and 'Sister Rose'
(*Household Words,* April 1855) and, most famously, Dickens' *A Tale
of Two Cities* (1859). As their collaborative relationship continued
to mature, the imaginative influence of one writer upon the other
was mutual.

The Frozen Deep performances in early January of 1857 took
place just as Collins was launching his new novel, *The Dead Secret*,
in the pages of *Household Words*. The feverish pace of his work
appears even more impressive when one considers that he was
working in multiple genres for the overlapping projects. Writing
his portions of *The Wreck of the Golden Mary* while also working

on *The Frozen Deep* and *The Dead Secret*, Collins was composing a short story to frame a Christmas number, a play in which he also performed, and a novel in weekly parts. *The Dead Secret* was his first serialised full-length novel, and from January to June of 1857, its instalments were also the first pieces in *Household Words* carrying an author's name other than Dickens'. The stress of protracted weekly deadlines for printers in England as well as the United States, where instalments appeared first in *Harper's Weekly*, was not only new but also fatiguing for Collins.

The Dead Secret mixes many elements of the Gothic – hauntings, old documents discovered in the abandoned wing of a great old house – with the shocking coincidences and revelation of family secrets characteristic of sensation fiction. It is perhaps most complicated in its exploration of co-dependencies and powerful loyalties between servants and employers. On her deathbed, Mrs Treverton demands that her servant, Sarah Leeson, write and sign a document explaining that the child known as Rosamond Treverton was born of Sarah Leeson, not Mrs Treverton. In a successful attempt to regain her husband's attentions after the couple cannot conceive their own child, Mrs Treverton contrives to pass off Sarah Leeson's baby as her own when Mr Treverton is at sea, relieving the infant and Sarah, whose fiancé is killed by a falling rock in a mine, from the social stigma of a birth outside marriage. The deception tortures Sarah, turning her hair white, and she flees from the household after hiding the letter of confession in the Myrtle Room. Concealing the letter follows Mrs Treverton's orders that Sarah not destroy it or remove it from Porthgenna Tower, but Sarah denies her mistress' wish that Mr Treverton learn the full truth. The eventual discovery of the secret also depends upon whether a servant will remain loyal. Because Leeson removes the labels from the keys to the deserted wing of the house, the location of the Myrtle Room remains a mystery until Rosamond's uncle's servant, Shrowl, secretly forwards the architectural plans. A servant trafficking in his master's secrets for financial gain was a bourgeois nightmare, yet readers here root for such betrayal. The plot's resolution depends on a servant crossing his employer in order to reveal a secret that exists because another servant crosses her employer by *not* revealing the secret. The novel, then, ultimately shows the embedded contradictions produced by servants' intimate positions in families.

Rosamond Treverton's curiosity foreshadows the women detective figures in Collins' later novels and builds upon 'The Diary of Anne Rodway' (*Household Words*, July 1856), in which Collins created the first fictional woman detective figure in a short story. Knowing only that a strange servant – Sarah Leeson in disguise – warns her away from the Myrtle Room, Rosamond is as determined to locate it as she is devoted to her husband, Leonard Frankland, whose loss of sight makes him no less dear to her. Collins' portrayal of blindness is not as thorough as his later explorations of the condition; here, he is more interested in Rosamond's reaction to the blindness than the experience of blindness itself. Given the opportunity to break their engagement when Leonard loses his sight completely, Rosamond chooses to stay with him. When Rosamond reads the letter containing the secret of her birth, it is Leonard's blindness that prevents her from destroying the letter because she cannot stomach the thought of taking advantage of his dependency. Rosamond's revelation of her actual parentage to a husband who has been raised to value rank highly also serves as an outlet for Collins to comment on the power of storytelling. After failing to persuade Leonard to play along with a hypothetical statement of her situation, Rosamond draws him into the scenario by positing it as the plot of a novel she might like to write. She repeatedly asks, 'How would you end it, love?' (Bk V, Ch VI). Collins' metatextual reflection here highlights the slippage between art and life, for Leonard's response will determine the conclusion to both Rosamond's and Collins' stories.

Collins followed the novel's modest success with a move back to the stage, and August of 1857 brought important developments to his theatrical career. Most significantly, one of Collins' plays was produced professionally for the first time. On 10th August, the Olympic Theatre staged *The Lighthouse*, which Dickens had produced privately two years prior. The play, based on Collins' own 'Gabriel's Marriage', was a hit, filling the Olympic's house for over eight weeks. Collins was thrilled to have famous figures, such as Thackeray and Dickens, in attendance and observed publicly as admirers of his work. Also in August, Dickens worked up a benefit performance of *The Frozen Deep* for the family of Douglas Jerrold, a recently deceased friend and playwright with whom Collins had also been very close. In the staging of *The Frozen Deep* for a public audience in Manchester, Charley Collins joined the cast, and Dickens replaced his women relatives with professional actresses. One of them, the eighteen-year-old Ellen Ternan, infatuated him for the rest of his life. Within a year, Dickens had separated rather indiscreetly from Catherine, his wife of two decades, and had started to maintain Miss Ternan, more or less secretly, as his companion.

A remarkable testament to the strength of his friendship with Dickens, Collins remained friendly with both Charles and Catherine. Dickens had urged his friends, associates, and even his children either to support his handling of the separation unequivocally, cutting Catherine Dickens from their circles of acquaintance, or to forfeit his professional and personal company. Collins was a rare exception. Not only did he continue to visit Catherine, his signature to a letter of 7th April 1862 repeatedly expresses his affection:

> With kind regards,
> Believe me
> My dear Mrs Dickens
> very truly yours
> Wilkie Collins

Collins may have felt the need to emphasise that 'dear Mrs Dickens' had not slipped a bit in his estimation because, even before the completion of the separation, he had assisted Dickens in finding ways to see Ternan.

Collins' presence provided extra cover when, once *The Frozen Deep* had concluded, Dickens was so miserable away from Ternan that he followed her to Doncaster under the pretext of reporting on the famous races for *Household Words*. The two writers set out on a walking tour of Cumberland in September of 1857, and their narrative of the adventures, *The Lazy Tour of Two Idle Apprentices* (*Household Words*, October 1857), is a fascinating example of how the collaborators textualised their voices as well as their bodies. As Thomas Idle and Francis Goodchild respectively, Collins and Dickens wittily satirise themselves, trading barbs on the merits of indolence versus industry among other things. After several misadventures, the frustrated Idle demands that they retire to an inn known for its special daily desserts: 'Let us eat Bride-cake without the trouble of being married, or of knowing anybody in that ridiculous dilemma.' Poking fun at a marital situation Dickens himself had made 'ridiculous', Collins was not immune from jest. Having badly sprained his ankle on an ill-advised climb through rain and fog up Carrock Fell, a lamed Collins needed Dickens' help to descend the remote mountain. Although Dickens' insistence upon taking the hike in bad weather had got them into the scrape in the first place, his portion teasingly describes Idle being 'melodramatically carried to the inn's first floor' after the ordeal. *The Lazy Tour* also contains Collins' chilling tale of a man who agrees to share a room with a corpse that not only comes to life but also turns out to be his half-brother. The sensational Gothic piece later appeared as 'Brother Morgan's Story of the Dead Hand' in *Queen of Hearts*, a collection of previously published stories that Collins published with a loose connecting framework in 1859.

The collaborative process was pleasing enough that Collins and Dickens quickly followed *The Lazy Tour* with another joint work. For *The Perils of Certain English Prisoners* (1857), Dickens chose for the first time to call upon no contributors other than

Collins for the *Household Words* Christmas number. The number constituted a response to the Indian Rebellion, which had begun on 10th May. Multiple factors led to the violent agitation for independence, and the trigger that began this incident of blood shedding concerned the greasing of ammunition cartridges, which had to be opened with one's teeth, with pig and cow fats. An Indian soldier, or sepoy, opening a cartridge was thereby forced to violate orthodox Muslim or Hindu beliefs. The British public was outraged to learn that some women and children were killed in the insurrection, and British military forces spent the next year re-establishing power at all costs, sometimes slaughtering entire Indian villages. Dickens' reaction, possibly fuelled by concern for his son Walter who headed to India in July for military service, matched the hyperbolically fierce tones of the British citizenry. Collins' reaction was less extreme. Their fictional commentary shifts the setting to South America and the year to 1744. Still, the story of English colonisers held hostage by 'native' pirates undeniably speaks to contemporary matters. Collins' chapter attempts not to erase but to lessen the ferocity of the number's racism with a tone far more comic than Dickens'. The doubling prevalent in both Collins' and Dickens' other works of the period appears here in Marion Maryon, one of the leaders of the British escape attempt whose savvy wielding of weapons helps endear her to the story's hero. Collins was not convinced that his contribution to *Perils* provided enough of, or the right type of, response to the rebellion, so he followed it up with 'A Sermon for Sepoys' in *Household Words* on 27th February 1858. Anticipating *The Moonstone*, this short essay reminds readers of the long and respectable history of non-Christian religious beliefs, working against mainstream depictions of Indians as hopelessly ruthless savages.

Collins spent much of 1858 writing excellent and sometimes groundbreaking journalism. 'Who is the Thief?' published in *The Atlantic Monthly* in April of 1858, is recognised as the first comical detective story as well as the first told in epistolary form.

The correspondence of Sergeant Bulmer, Chief Inspector Theak-stone, and Matthew Sharpin shows Mr Sharpin to be an arrogant law clerk whose rookie assignment on the detective force stems from high connections in the London detective office. Sharpin, a 'conceited booby', energetically pursues the wrong suspect while investigating a theft case until Theakstone intercedes to appre-hend the actual thief, whose identity emerges plainly in Sharpin's oblivious letters. The story is now most frequently called 'The Biter Bit' because it appeared later as 'Brother Griffith's Story of The Biter Bit' in *Queen of Hearts*. Collins' humour treats a different subject in 'The Unknown Public' (*Household Words*, 21st August 1858). Assuming the voice of an implausibly naive discoverer of weekly penny journals, whose readership he esti-mates at three million, he alerts his comrades in the 'literary world' to the existence of these masses who await instruction on how to distinguish between good and bad writing. Ironically, one complaint Collins voices about the novels published in these journals – that they are often 'a combination of fierce melodrama and meek domestic sentiment' – is a charge critics would levy against his own later novels. The public Collins thought he knew well disappointed him in October of 1858, when his new play, *The Red Vial*, debuted dismally at the Olympic Theatre. Particularly irritated by things like a reanimated corpse whose death-like appearance was caused by a slow-acting poison antidote, critics and audiences showed no mercy in their rejection of the bleak work, and Collins did his best to recover by making sure that no copies of the play found their way into print.

The year ended with Collins working hard on another col-laborative Christmas number, *A House to Let*, and also sharing his friend's contemplation of an enormous change in domestic arrangements. While Dickens was fumbling through a marital separation that he hoped would not destroy his public reputation or force him to give up his mistress, Wilkie had found a love inter-est of his own. Caroline Graves was born Elizabeth Compton, but she went by several different names in her lifetime. She was born around 1830, a date difficult to pin down because she often understated her age. Beautiful and proud, it was easy for her to convince others that she was younger than her actual years. She had been married to George Robert Graves, a clerk, for less than two years when he died of tuberculosis in 1852. Left with a one-year-old daughter, Elizabeth Harriet, Caroline survived by keeping a small shop in London, and she probably had baby-minding help from her mother-in-law Mrs Graves, to whom she and Harriet always remained close. Wilkie Collins lived near the shop for a time, which suggests that they met in the neighbour-hood between 1854 and 1856. By late 1858, perhaps earlier, Wilkie, Caroline, and little Harriet were keeping house together. Wilkie immediately treated Harriet, whom he called 'Carrie', as his own daughter, she regarded him as a loving father, and he made sure she received an education.

For the rest of Collins' life, with the exception of one brief separation, he shared a home with Caroline as his unmarried companion. He often railed against the institution of marriage, not only in his fiction but also in his journalism, including a 13th December 1856 piece for *Household Words* titled 'Bold Words by a Bachelor', and no evidence suggests that he was ever tempted to wed Caroline. No letters between Wilkie and Caroline sur-vive to illuminate the terms of the relationship. Wilkie regularly mentioned her as he would a wife in letters to his friends, and he seemed untroubled by the fact that taking up residence with his lover flew in the face of their society's articulated sexual values. They were open about the relationship to all of their friends, some of whom were notable unmarried couples such as George Eliot (Mary Ann Evans) and George Lewes, who had brazenly set up house together in defiance of public disapproval. Wilkie and Caroline took a middle path, living together unmar-ried yet retaining a 'cover' story in which Caroline sometimes took the name 'Mrs Collins' or assumed the identity of Collins' 'housekeeper'. Although they travelled together and entertained as a couple at their home, Caroline was not invited to join Wilkie at the home of his good friends Fred and Nina Lehmann or at Dickens', where her presence as an open mistress would have compromised respectability. Collins' mother Harriet appears to have taken a hard line on the affair. No surviving letter of Wilkie to Harriet mentions the existence of Caroline or Carrie, and no existing evidence suggests that the two ever met. Harriet's seemingly complete rejection of her son's new family suggests that the moralistic views of her husband had not completely vanished.

Speculations about the reasons for Collins' decision to remain unmarried range from the idea that a youthful heartbreak set him against marriage forever to notions that an early engagement or entanglement left him unable to marry legally. It may also simply be that Collins truly opposed the reasoning behind the institution. Always critical of husbands' abilities to control and profit from the bodies and fortunes of their wives, Collins was consistent when he refused to assume the legal position of a husband himself. He was critical of both sides of the arrangement. One of his later heroines, Valeria Macallan, graces the final chapter of *The Law and the Lady* with the following proclamation about women who marry simply for money: 'When a woman sells herself to a man, that vile bargain is none the less infamous (to my mind), because it happens to be made under the sanction of the Church and the Law.' Drawing direct comparisons between marriage and prostitution throughout his career, Collins clearly felt that living with a mistress instead of a wife actually placed him further away from the role of a pimp.

Collins may have spurned marriage, but he definitely did not evade responsibility or even commitment. His dedication to Caroline's and Carrie's welfare never wavered. His position seems to have been a consistent rejection of an institution regulated by perverse, oppressive, and inconsistent laws meant to restrict rather than to nurture loving relationships and the unpredictable force of human passion. By the age of thirty-four,

Wilkie was suddenly the head of his own small family, with a woman other than his mother presiding over his domestic affairs and comforts. Never again would Collins be unattached or at the centre of the type of bachelor lifestyle he had prized for so long. In fact, over the years ahead, his family would continue to grow.

The 1860s: A Decade of Distinction

The novels Collins published in the 1860s are the best and most enduring of his career. *The Woman in White, No Name, Armadale*, and *The Moonstone*, written in less than a full decade, show Collins not just as a master of his craft but also as an innovator and provocateur. These four works, which secured him an international reputation and sold in large numbers, ensured his financial stability and allowed him to support many others. As Collins composed the novels and enjoyed their popularity, he also continued to experience severe attacks of rheumatic gout and other maladies. Often debilitated, he did not resign himself to suffering. Rather, he continued to doggedly pursue treatments that would alleviate the condition and hopefully decrease his dependence on opium. Not content to become an ageing invalid in his late thirties and early forties, Collins maintained old friendships, initiated new romances, and challenged himself artistically.

Collins' four great novels showcase carefully constructed plot twists while also displaying impressive range in narrative form and theme. Some topics, such as the loss of a woman's legal rights upon marriage and the significance of dreams, continually resurface but not always in predictable ways. The novels' scenarios question the ways in which murderers become sympathetic, the moral significance of prolonged infirmity, and whether it is possible to distinguish between identity theft and harmless impersonation. Elements of mystery and detection force readers into the action of the plots with an increased awareness of their own roles as makers of meaning. As Collins explains in his prefaces, sometimes he focuses on how strong-willed characters affect circumstances, and at other times he explores how circumstance affects character. He therefore avoids settling into the same manner of exploring the central questions that preoccupy him. Instead, he comes at a favourite issue from a new direction, or flips the perspective and positioning of his protagonists. The nearly suicidal Magdalen Vanstone in *No Name* tells a story entirely different from the actually suicidal Rosanna Spearman in *The Moonstone*. Altered states of consciousness, whether due to the effects of disturbed sleep, dreams or drugs, reappear to equally intriguing yet varied effect in several works. Adventures in foreign lands might rehabilitate a weak hero, as in *The Woman in White*, or threaten multiple generations of a landed family, as in *Armadale*. Whether developing increasingly complicated mixed race characters or imagining intimate bonds that challenge conventional sexuality, Collins' most famous works also employ a variety of narrative devices. His methods, sometimes including fictional historical documents, sometimes using an omniscient narrator to communicate the scheming thoughts of multiple characters, and sometimes using up to eleven different narrators, enable the novels to achieve extraordinary effects.

The writing of *The Woman in White* commenced at Broadstairs in the summer of 1859, when Collins was also dealing with some particularly uncomfortable health problems. Writing to Charles Ward on 30th August, he complained, 'I have been suffering torments with a b<u>oil</u> <u>between</u> my legs, and write these lines with the agreeable prospect of the doctor coming to lance it. I seem destined, God help me!, never to be well.' The possibility of venereal disease seems particularly likely here, as the affliction appears to have returned in October. Again writing to Ward, Wilkie explained, 'I have had my old torment in the sac since I saw you and have never stirred outside the door' (20th/27th October 1859). The word 'sac' is difficult to decipher in Collins' hand. Some editors have read it as 'ear', but Peters' reading of the word as 'sac' appears more intuitive, given that Collins did not suffer from regular ailments of the ear and that his letter of six weeks earlier specifically laments a between-the-legs affliction. Despite the distress of the boil, he worked on *The Woman in White* every day.

This particular plot Collins designed extensively beforehand, even outlining it on paper, but the actual drafting remained very challenging. The difficulty was not that he had to decide what was going to happen; it was a matter of working out details and crafting language to achieve the suspense exactly as he had envisioned. Because an immense amount of timing and fine points of law had to be correct in order for the plot to cohere, Collins' legal training and those years he spent revelling in the dinners at Lincoln's Inn served him well. His skill at keeping legal minutiae straight and presenting complicated cases comprehensibly, which reappears in his later works, set *The Woman in White* apart.

The inspiration for *The Woman in White* came from Maurice Méjan's *Recueil des Causes Célèbres* (1808), a book Collins had picked up on one of his trips to Paris with Dickens. Collins decided to recast Méjan's account of Madame de Douhault, whose own brother legally established her death by imprisoning her in a madhouse with a false identity in 1788. He and another male relative stole Madame de Douhault's fortune, and she was never able to regain her true identity even after escaping from the asylum. Madame de Douhault becomes Laura Fairlie in *The Woman in White*, and the villain is her husband, Sir Percival Glyde. Fairlie weds Glyde to satisfy a promise to her deceased father even though she has fallen in love with Walter Hartright, her drawing teacher. To secure Laura's fortune, Glyde takes advantage of her likeness to another woman, Anne Catherick, by sending Laura to a madhouse under Catherick's identity and burying the corpse of the real Anne Catherick in a grave marked with Laura's name.

Laura's passive qualities leave her dependent upon her strong-willed half-sister, Marian Halcombe, and Walter Hartright.

Marian stands out as one of Collins' most assertive and active women. She strips off 'white and cumbersome' undergarments in favour of a sleeker costume that permits her to creep along a verandah roof in the rain so that she may eavesdrop on her sister's enemies, and she later finds and frees Laura from the asylum (Second Epoch, Ch IX). The tireless efforts of Walter Hartright, who continues to love Laura, expose Glyde's conspiracy. Assisted by a perfectly eccentric Italian villain in the form of Count Fosco, Glyde turns out to be concealing far more secrets than the faked death of his wife, and the brilliance of the plot is that it revolves around multiple mysteries. The story is centred not only on whose machinations will triumph but also on motive and the unravelling of the mystery behind Anne Catherick, the woman dressed in white whose abrupt, middle of the night confrontation with Hartright distinguishes the novel's early chapters.

Walter Hartright is also a key figure in the development of Collins' narrative techniques. The opening paragraphs present Walter as the person arranging the documents that comprise the novel, and he immediately establishes a level of credibility that not only replaces but also trumps 'the machinery of the Law'. With more integrity than an actual court of law, 'the pre-engaged servant of the long purse', Hartright authorises himself by banning hearsay and justifying his own occasional narration. Swiftly pulling the reader into a story told through a web of documents, Collins is so confident in his method that he playfully closes the 'Second Epoch' with multiple narratives, including one from an illiterate cook and one from 'the Tombstone'.

The Woman in White was an immediate and enormous success. Dickens had chosen to follow his own *A Tale of Two Cities* with Collins' novel to launch *All the Year Round* (formerly *Household Words*). Collins' novel skyrocketed sales of the journal from 26th November 1859 to 25th August 1860, and it was simultaneously serialised abroad in *Harper's Weekly* (New York). By the end of the 1850s, Collins was already a well-known author, but *The Woman in White* propelled him to a level of renown rivalled by few writers of the period. Margaret Oliphant penned a positive review, and other notable figures, such as William Makepeace Thackeray and William Gladstone (not yet Prime Minister), reportedly could not put the book down. It spawned songs, dances in the form of a waltz and the 'Fosco Galop', and even a perfume. A more lasting facet of the novel's legacy is the oft-repeated story that Caroline Graves, fleeing from some sort of madman or pimp into Wilkie's arms on the streets of London, was the original woman in white. John Everett Millais and Kate Dickens repeated Millais' father's account of such a story, but each of those sources is faulty on other matters of historical record, and nothing in Collins' own papers corroborates the story.

Following serialisation, the book's sales in three-volume form continued to grow. Whether hungering for an expensive early edition or a later 'cheap edition', the public's appetite seemed endless, and by November of 1860, *The Woman in White* was already in its eighth edition. In the meantime, an astute reviewer for *The Times* had noticed a chronological error that irritated Collins but that he was relieved to be able to correct, starting with the 1861 editions. In part because Collins had wisely retained the copyrights for his earlier novels, which were increasingly in demand, and in part because he profited from the translation of his works throughout the 1850s into multiple languages, including German, Russian and French, finances now ceased to be a concern. In the summer of 1860, Wilkie and Charley at last opened their own bank accounts and stopped relying on Harriet for their cash flow. Dickens was lucky enough to have already secured the successor to *The Woman in White* for publication in *All the Year Round*, but he was outbid by Smith and Elder when they offered Collins the astonishing sum of £5,000 to publish the following novel in *The Cornhill*, a more elite journal edited by Thackeray.

In the final weeks of July 1860, as Wilkie was finishing the last instalments of *The Woman in White*, Charley, aged thirty-two, married Dickens' twenty-year-old daughter Kate. The father of the bride was not overly pleased to have the sickly and weak Charles Collins for a son-in-law, but he might have been unhappy with any groom. He blamed his own domestic discord for Kate's decision to marry and reportedly wept over her wedding gown when she left the house. Wilkie was no more excited about his brother's nuptials than he was about any others, as he continued to detest the institution of marriage. The families' concerns were apparently validated; no dramatic scandals followed, but little joy accompanied the union, and the marriage may never have been consummated. Rumours and statements Kate made after Charley's death indicate that his physical ailments included impotence but that Kate, in accordance with her father's wishes, chose continued marriage over pursuing a legal separation on such grounds. Charley had been struggling for years to find peace with his identity as an artist. His insecurities only intensified with age, and he became paralysed before the canvas. By 1858, he had abandoned painting and earned his living by publishing short periodical pieces, often in *All the Year Round*. Dickens also accepted some of his contributions for every Christmas number in the 1860s save one. Remarkably, only the first four of the eighteen Christmas numbers Dickens produced are without a story by one or both of the Collins brothers.

Just a few months before Kate Dickens became Mrs Charles Collins, Caroline Graves had taken the name 'Mrs Collins' when she and Wilkie moved into 12 Harley Street. Of course, Caroline could not attend the wedding since she was not officially a 'Mrs' Collins, and the two women did not socialise as informal sisters-in-law. In October of 1860, 'Mr and Mrs' Wilkie Collins continued to celebrate *The Woman in White* with a lavish trip to Paris. Wilkie relaxed, enjoyed spending his money, revelled in celebrity, and was in no hurry to write more than a few pieces of journalism. Wilkie and Caroline were both charming personalities, and they maintained a warm circle of friends throughout their lives, including another unmarried couple: Charles Reade and Laura Seymour. Reade and Seymour, an actress, lived together and called Reade's son by another woman (who died in childbirth) his nephew. Collins and Reade became especially close even though Reade was a divisive figure whose sensation novels were not only scandalous but also frequently plagiarised from other works. Ironically, Reade was an ally of Collins and Dickens in fighting for stricter copyright laws. Among Reade and others, Wilkie was a popular guest who joked around pleasantly in awkward social situations to set people at ease, and his letters are full of entertaining ironies. He frequently fell ill and had to miss engagements, but when he did venture out, health complaints were suspended as Wilkie's presence buoyed the spirits of others.

Eventually, Collins began to outline ideas for a new novel, travelling domestically with Caroline to gather information for *No Name*. As he approached the writing of his next book, it was clear that his stature merited leaving his staff position at *All the Year Round*, and in January of 1862 there was no acrimony with Dickens over his departure. At the start of writing *No Name*, then, Collins was not overburdened with professional commitments, but rheumatism plagued him incessantly, forcing him to delay the publication schedule. Wilkie called nearly all of his ailments 'gout', and this episode involved severe affliction in his eyes. Peters has advanced speculation about Collins' potential ailment by suggesting that he may have been suffering from Reiter's disease, a reactive form of arthritis often triggered by chlamydia or gonorrhoea. Because one of the main symptoms of Reiter's disease is an inflammation of the eyes, Peters posits that Collins' future attacks point strongly to Reiter's rather than to simple rheumatic gout. It is important to recall, however, that Collins' father William also experienced what he called gout in the eyes, and little evidence indicates that William suffered from venereal disease. It is quite conceivable that Wilkie suffered from venereal disease and arthritis on top of an inherited ocular disease such as glaucoma. Whatever the cause, Collins nursed painfully inflamed red eyes that sometimes required bandages, and he dictated portions of *No Name* to Dr Francis Beard.

A friend as well as a medical attendant, Dr Beard did not hesitate to prescribe opium, and Collins expressed his gratitude to his amanuensis in the novel's dedication.

The first instalment of *No Name* appeared on 15th March 1862 in *All the Year Round* and *Harper's Weekly*. From July to October, Collins moved Caroline and Carrie to Broadstairs for a change of air as he continued writing. When he returned to London, his illness was so extreme that it threatened his completion of the last volume of the book. Collins had solicited substantial feedback from Dickens on the manuscript, variously taking and ignoring Dickens' advice, so when Collins worried that he would have to stop writing, Dickens valiantly offered to cut short his upcoming Paris trip in order to rescue the work. To his credit, Dickens' letter of 14th October sounds more like a genuine offer of help to a distressed friend than a patronising or self-congratulatory gesture. He suggested completing the instalments by reviewing and talking over Wilkie's notes, promising to write in a style 'so like you as that no one should find out the difference'. He also sought to reassure Collins by reminding him of their previous collaborations: 'Think it a Xmas No., an Idle apprentice, a Lighthouse, a Frozen Deep. I am as ready as in any of those cases to strike in and hammer the hot iron out.' To be sure, Dickens fretted about halting the publication of a novel appearing in the pages of his own journal, but his letter focused primarily on calming Collins, assuring him, 'You will be well (and thankless!) in no time. But here I am. And I hope that the knowledge may be a comfort to you. Call me, and I come.' Collins was not soon well, but Dr Beard kept him conscious enough to be able to finish the book himself by Christmas.

No Name is theatrical in its narration: the novel unfolds in eight 'Scenes' with documents, primarily in the form of letters, also appearing in sections 'Between the Scenes'. Because each 'scene' is presented by an omniscient rather than a first-person narrator, the novel differs more in style from *The Woman in White* than its form initially suggests. No character takes the place of Walter

Hartright as drawer of scenes, making *No Name* more traditional as a novel shaped by an unseen hand for the reader's pleasure. The plot differs substantially from *The Woman in White* as well. Whereas *The Woman in White* took up the hazards of marriage, *No Name* worries about the dangers of not marrying. Magdalen and Norah Vanstone grow up in a stable family, but when their loving parents suddenly die, the girls discover that Mr and Mrs Vanstone were not legally married until after the girls' births. Because Mr Vanstone dies on his way to draw up a new will, his brother Michael Vanstone is able to deprive the sisters of any inheritance. The fact that the Vanstones did legally marry before they died does nothing to legitimise, or to provide a 'name' for, Magdalen and Norah.

As foreshadowed by her multiple roles in a private theatrical performance of *The Rivals* (which Collins knew well, having enjoyed his own amateur production of it at Blandford Square), Magdalen initially supports herself by taking to the stage. Later, she schemes to marry a repellent cousin on her quest to regain the unjustly lost inheritance and also repeatedly impersonates people, which calls attention to the performance of gentility on a larger scale. The ease with which Magdalen can switch places with Louisa, a maid, raises the alarming possibility that the reverse process would also be simple. Such cross-class posturing was a hallmark of sensation fiction that had already appeared in Collins' *The Dead Secret* as well as Mrs Henry Wood's *East Lynne* (1861), and *No Name*'s sensational characteristics pleased readers if not reviewers, many of whom were dissatisfied with the moral standing of Collins' heroine and the resolution of the plot. It was extremely transgressive for the novel to sympathetically portray the Vanstones leading a fake married family life with Mr Vanstone's first wife still alive in Canada. In an August 1863 review for *Blackwood's*, Margaret Oliphant, who had heaped praise upon *The Woman in White* for the plausibility of its shocking moments, lambasted Magdalen Vanstone as a polluted heroine, guilty of 'vulgar and aimless trickery and wickedness, with which it is impossible to have a shadow of sympathy'. Yet even reviewers who were most outraged at the novel's immorality and who regarded Magdalen as a 'perverse heroine', to quote H.F. Chorley writing for *The Athenaeum* on 3rd January 1863, felt compelled to acknowledge Collins' supreme narrative skill and mastery of creating suspense in the serial form. Those qualities mattered most to readers, and *No Name* continues to be regarded as one of Collins' best novels.

Even with its theatrical framing, Collins was never able to stage *No Name* successfully, and he was in no shape to take on such a production when he had finished writing. Having barely managed to finish the novel, Collins spent most of 1863 travelling to undergo treatments that might cure his gout and what had become a serious addiction to opium. Even after accounting for possible exaggeration in the accounts of his alarmed friends, Collins had advanced well beyond the normal levels of heightened tolerance that occur with habitual use of narcotics. He was dosing himself with amounts of opium that would have killed most people. Increasingly, he struggled to balance the laudanum's palliative effects with the side effects of hallucinations and nightmares. He used other remedies, including quinine and potassium, not only for the gout pains but also to address the opium's disruption of his digestion and nerves. Add alcohol to the mix, and one can easily understand why his case became so difficult to manage. Collins never broke his addiction to opium, but he was able to decrease his use over some periods of time. In 1863, he threw himself into trying to recover and admirably maintained his hopes through the fluctuating results of various therapies. In January, his feet were in such poor condition that he could not walk down a flight of stairs. Under the treatment of Dr Beard and, for a time, Dr John Elliotson, he and Caroline tried several methods to ease his pain, including mesmerism. At first, the hypnosis produced positive results, and, as intended, weaned Collins off opium, but its effects were not long-lasting. In the spring, he and Caroline were planning a trip to explore some treatments abroad when they were upset to hear that Augustus Egg, Collins' senior by just seven and a half years, had died from chronic lung problems. Collins wrote to Beard, 'Nothing can replace the loss – he was a man in ten thousand. It is a calamity, in every sense of the word, for everyone who knew him' (4th April 1863). With the loss of Egg augmenting Collins' desire to prevent his own chronic ailments from gaining the upper hand, Wilkie and Caroline headed to medical men in Germany.

Their target destinations were the baths at Aix-la-Chapelle and Wildbad. In his letters to Harriet, Wilkie not only explains the treatments but also indulges her maternal pride by sharing his pleasure at finding photographers and autograph seekers eagerly courting him. The sulphurous water at Aix-la-Chapelle smelled and tasted awful, but the combination of cool and warm water treatments, hot linen wraps, and a diet of good food and wine had a continuously positive effect. Collins' good humour during the visit is evident in his letters, particularly in anecdotes about his German attendant, with whom he could only converse in French while shouting over the water. Writing to Nina Lehmann, Wilkie chuckled over their linguistic challenges: 'In mistakes of gender, I am well ahead of the German – it being an old habit of mine, and of my love and respect for the fair sex, to make all French words about the gender of which I feel uncertain, feminine words. But in other respects my German friend is beyond me. This great creature has made an entirely new discovery in the science of language – he does without Verbs' (29th April 1863).

Although the remedies at Aix-la-Chapelle seemed effective, Collins decided to head to the hot springs at Wildbad, which were far more pleasing to the nose but increased his pain significantly. The doctor prescribed twenty-four baths and was confident of the long-term benefit of the method, even if Wilkie departed for home feeling temporarily worse. The treatment was a sort of purge – bringing out the rheumatic pain in order to expunge it – that may have been a costly mistake. Returning to

England in June, Wilkie was excited about the prospect of taking a cruise with Pigott in July, but as soon as he was on the yacht, he felt worse. After ten days of toughing out severe back pain, Wilkie turned back and resigned himself to having to leave England for the winter. His plan was to stop at the Isle of Man to collect some information for his next book, then to head to Italy. Refusing to lose hope, he wrote to Harriet on 4th August 1863, 'Don't be downhearted about me. I sleep better than I did, and I am not at all out of spirits... Nothing shakes my resolution to pull myself through this mess – and you will see I shall do it.' He also did not worry about the lengthy pause between novels, realising that he needed strength to be able to work: 'I am not forty yet – and I can afford to wait.'

When Collins did turn forty, his spirits remained high. Writing to Harriet from Rome on his birthday and adding to the header of his letter 'Feast of St Collins', he exclaimed:

> *Mercy on us! Who would ever have thought it. Here is 'forty' come upon me – grey hairs springing fast, especially about the temples – rheumatism and gout familiar enemies for some time past – all the worst signs of middle-age sprouting out on me – and yet, in spite of it all, I don't feel old. I have no regular habits, no respectable prejudices, no tendency to go to sleep after dinner, no loss of appetite for public amusements, none of the melancholy sobrieties of sentiment, in short, which are supposed to be proper to middle age. Surely, there is some mistake? Are you and I really as old as you suppose? Do review your past recollections, and see whether you are quite sure that there is no miscalculation and no mistake.*

> *– 8th January 1864*

A vivid illustration of Collins' positive attitude and youthful humour, his musings also remind us that feeling healthy was an exceptional occasion for most of his life. The tone of his letters to Harriet indicates a close relationship and even friendship between mother and son, but Caroline's presence obviously had caused some splintering in the family. Wilkie wrote to his mother as if Caroline did not exist. Given that he had also happily assumed a paternal role for Carrie, Harriet was absent from the central relationships of his life.

The contrast between Wilkie's letters to Harriet and his letters to other friends is striking. To Charles Ward on 4th November 1863, he explains that Caroline and Carrie were overcome with seasickness on a visit to Civita Vecchia and that Caroline 'was so ill that she could not be moved from the deck all night, and she has hardly got over the effect of the voyage yet'. Yet he writes to Harriet in the first person, as if he is completely alone: 'Thus far, I have kept myself to myself – and I doubt if anybody in Rome knows I am here. Ideas are coming to me thicker & thicker for a new book – and while I am putting them down and considering and re-considering them "company" only distracts and worries me. I think I am going to hit on a rather extraordinary story this time – something entirely different from anything I have done yet' (4th December 1863). Wilkie certainly did not swear off the 'company' of Caroline and her daughter, and, even with the episode of seasickness, their companionship did not hinder his inspiration.

Feeling somewhat restored to health and able to take walks for pleasure, Collins increasingly contemplated and plotted the story for his next novel but did not begin writing *Armadale* until he returned to England in March. In August of 1864, he was well enough to sail to the Norfolk Broads, where he did more scouting for the book with Pigott and Charles Ward. The complex plot involves two men with the name of Allan Armadale. One goes by that name and the other is called Ozias Midwinter. When Midwinter comes of age, he receives his father's deathbed confession: a lengthy document explaining that he murdered Allan Armadale's father and forbidding contact between the two younger men who share that name. Midwinter ignores the warning without sharing any of the information with Allan, who has rather improbably become a close friend. A series of dreams and visions create suspense around whether the friendship of the two Allan Armadales can survive and lead them to happiness or whether the men's acquaintance will lead them to ruin.

The figure of Midwinter is intriguing on many fronts. He is Collins' first major novelistic mixed race character. Midwinter's father, born in Barbados to an English family, married a woman of European and African descent whom he met in Trinidad. When Midwinter's temper flares, the novel attributes the rage to the 'hot' Creole blood and 'savage' nature he inherited from his mother, yet his time growing up with a 'gipsy' man seems to have formed his character more forcefully, which raises the question of whether or not Midwinter's racial difference is truly essentialised. Furthermore, the passionate feelings that align Midwinter with Creole stereotypes are the same feelings that make him heroic. In addition to constantly existing as a racial other, Midwinter is feminised, and his relationship with Armadale has strong homo-erotic overtones. Midwinter's love for Armadale is so intense that he breaks down in a 'hysterical passion' even contemplating a separation (Bk II, Ch II). When he observes Allan dreaming, 'Midwinter laid his hand gently on Allan's forehead. Light as the touch was, there were mysterious sympathies in the dreaming man that answered it. His groaning ceased, and his hands dropped slowly. There was an instant of suspense, and Midwinter looked closer. His breath just fluttered over the sleeper's face' (Bk II, Ch IV). Here, the intimate 'sympathies' between the two men, which seem nearly to prompt a kiss, are calming and provide relief as opposed to turmoil.

The novel's other central figure, and one of Collins' most nuanced character studies, is Lydia Gwilt. The complexity of Gwilt's character, which repulsed reviewers, also marks the novel's impressive psychological depth. Knowing that Midwinter must sign his true name on a marriage certificate, Gwilt marries him then conspires to have Armadale killed abroad so that she can inherit his fortune as the widowed Mrs Armadale. After scandalously manipulating appearances so that neighbours will believe Allan really did marry her, Gwilt puts the murderous plan into action, separates herself from Midwinter, and returns to England as Armadale's widow. When she encounters Midwinter, she fells him by coldly denying that she is his wife. At this moment of heightened cruelty, when one expects her to appear most vilified, she remains human:

> With both arms clasped round him, the miserable woman lifted his lifeless face to hers, and rocked him on her bosom in an agony of tenderness beyond all relief in tears, in a passion of remorse beyond all expression in words. In silence she held him to her breast, in silence she devoured his forehead, his cheeks, his lips, with kisses. Not a sound escaped her, till she heard the trampling footsteps outside, hurrying up the stairs. Then a low moan burst from her lips, as she looked her last at him, and lowered his head again to her knee, before the strangers came in. (Book the Last, Ch II)

By the novel's end, its femme fatale has struggled so mightily with her conscience that she is an object of pity. Even though she has killed or tried to kill more than one of her husbands, her love for Midwinter remains somewhat redemptive.

The Cornhill published the first instalment of *Armadale* in November of 1864, and American serialisation in *Harper's Monthly Magazine* was only one month behind. The effects of the American Civil War were threatening to ruin *Harper's* when *Armadale's* appearance bolstered its sales enough to keep it in business. *Armadale* was popular, but critics, as Collins had expected, balked at its moral posture, and the murderous Lydia Gwilt outraged reviewers even more than Magdalen Vanstone had. Collins finished the book in April of 1866 and immediately published a dramatic version to secure his copyright, but it was not performed. Collins also remained mobile in the mid-1860s despite the persistent gout attacks, taking two short trips to France and a longer trip with Pigott to Italy between 1865 and '66. In September of 1867, he faced the onerous task of moving house again.

Gloucester Place would be his home for the next two decades. In the beautiful and spacious house, Caroline and Wilkie were known for hosting elaborate dinners, and Wilkie was scrupulous in his culinary tastes. He wrote to Henry Pigott, 'Thank you for the asparagus – the only asparagus worth eating, to my mind, is the small green kind which you have kindly sent. Cold, with salad oil, is <u>my</u> way of doing justice to that delicate vegetable' (21st February 1886). Caroline's cooking also delighted Wilkie's friends; he reported that Edward Pigott asked her specifically to send the 'strong meat jelly which we make with a French machine' (15th March 1886). Carrie, in her mid-teens, enjoyed life at Gloucester Place, which would be her home until her marriage in 1878. The family was also fond of pets, and Collins especially doted on their Scottish terrier, Tommie. The initial move, though, was ill-timed, as the end of 1867 was extremely busy for Collins. He again managed multiple overlapping projects in various genres. Simultaneously, he was researching, plotting, and writing his next serial novel, *The Moonstone*; collaborating with Dickens on a new Christmas number, *No Thoroughfare*; dramatising *No Thoroughfare* for a stage production; and, beginning in November, helping to edit and manage the publication of *All the Year Round* while Dickens travelled to the United States. In this overcommitted period of time, Collins produced some of the most successful works of his career.

For *No Thoroughfare*, Dickens wanted the final Christmas number he produced to contain writing from only himself and Collins, like *The Perils of Certain English Prisoners* ten years before. They worked together in person at Gad's Hill and collaborated closely via letters for months, beginning in July. The story revolves around George Vendale's courtship of Marguerite Obenreizer and an intriguing revelation of mistaken identity that originates with Vendale's business partner, Walter Wilding. Having learned that a foundling hospital named her infant Walter Wilding, his mother, now able to care for him, returns about twelve years later to adopt him. After she dies, Wilding discovers that her actual son was adopted after just three months at the foundling hospital and that the staff had recycled the name. Feeling that he inherited his fortune wrongfully, and unable to cope with the revelation that the woman who loved him 'as only a mother could' was not his biological mother, Wilding wastes away and dies. George Vendale and another adviser promise to give his fortune to the first Walter Wilding should he be found within two years. Full of streets with no literal thoroughfares and moral conundrums with no meta-phorical thoroughfares leading to solutions, the rest of the story tracks Vendale. Vendale's goal is to identify a swindler who has defrauded his wine trading firm while also raising enough money to secure Marguerite's hand in marriage, freeing her from the oppressive authority of her uncle, Mr Jules Obenreizer. In a dra-matic journey to Switzerland, Obenreizer, the actual thief, thinks that he has murdered Vendale, but the nearly frozen man is res-cued by the astoundingly strong Marguerite, who materialises in the middle of a blizzard. Well outside the conventional role of a passive woman yet uniquely qualified to rescue Vendale on ac-count of her light frame, Marguerite demands that the rest of the rescue team lower her onto an ice shelf using a rope she master-fully ties about herself in complicated mountain climbing knots.

The story both invokes and mocks the sensation genre. Just after Walter learns that the first Walter Wilding was taken to Switzerland, a letter from that country arrives, and Obenreizer appears on the scene. The improbable coincidence leads readers to suspect that Obenreizer may be the first Walter Wilding, and his inexplicable behaviour coupled with strange events on their journey causes Vendale to suspect the same. The clumsy intro-duction of that possibility into the story feels like campy sensa-tion until readers are shocked by Obenreizer's revelation that George Vendale is the first Walter Wilding. In lieu of prosecut-ing Obenreizer for fraud and attempted murder, the major players avoid scandal by agreeing to let him go free if he will sign away authority over Marguerite. A timely *deus ex machina* rescues Collins and Dickens from having to justify such an alarmingly selfish disregard for public safety and justice: Obenreizer is crushed by an avalanche on his way out of Switzerland.

Written with the intentionally dramatic structure of an overture and three acts, *No Thoroughfare* easily moved from page to stage. Collins was thrilled to have Charles Fechter, a noted French actor who had come to London, as well as his frequent co-star Carlotta Leclercq take the lead roles. Fechter was brilliant, and the production, which opened on 26th December 1867 at the Adelphi Theatre, was the stage success that had eluded Collins for the past ten years. The *Red Vial* debacle in 1858 had counterbalanced *The Lighthouse*, and a professional production for which Collins had tweaked the script of *The Frozen Deep* in October of 1866 had not been received well. *No Thoroughfare*, by contrast, lasted a very profitable two hundred nights at the Adelphi before touring. Dickens worked with Fechter to write another stage adaptation for a Paris production, but it was terribly inferior to Collins'.

Many have speculated about a cooling in the Collins/Dickens friendship, particularly after the marriage of Charley and Kate, but it is difficult to determine whether such a rift existed or how deep it may have been. The older men each helped subsidise Charley's household, Dickens more begrudgingly than Collins, but Dickens' complaints in letters to other friends about Wilkie's attitude towards Charley must be considered with the understanding that letters often serve to diffuse and release frustrated feelings in place of direct confrontation. Almost none of the letters Collins wrote to Dickens have been preserved. Some of the evidence culled from surviving correspondence that has raised suspicion includes Collins' request that Dickens write a formal statement clarifying that Collins held the copyright to everything he published in *Household Words* and *All the Year Round*, which Dickens did on 27th January 1870. Dickens also expressed a wish to visit Collins, whom he had not seen for a while. These statements, particularly in isolation, cannot establish the existence of a severe falling out. There are countless reasonable causes for Collins to have desired written clarification of his copyright, and many of Collins' closest friends were unable to visit him when he was in very poor health. Close collaboration on *No Thoroughfare* in 1867, just a few years before Dickens' death, suggests an enduring artistic sympathy and solid trust between the writers at the very least. Collins continued to show Dickens early drafts of his novels, following his usual practice of considering without necessarily incorporating all suggested changes. Furthermore, beginning in November of 1867, Collins agreed to help Wills with the editorial duties at *All the Year Round* while Dickens was in the United States, and *The Moonstone* appeared in its pages beginning 4th January 1868.

Collins' excitement at the launch of *The Moonstone* was immediately checked when his mother, now seventy-seven years of age, fell ill in mid-January. Charley had been increasingly ill as well. As Harriet was dying, Wilkie suffered his most intense attack of gout yet in early February. Emotional stress and accumulated fatigue from the overlapping projects seem to have combined to help trigger the event. The condition affected his eyes to such an extent that he was unable to write or even to read. He was so ill that he could not visit Harriet immediately before her death on 19th March 1868, and he was devastated that he missed his own mother's funeral. Continuing work on the novel was a welcome distraction for Wilkie, and the extent to which extreme pain disabled him is not clear. Wilkie exaggerated his difficulties to his publishers, claiming that he dictated parts of the novel that are written in his own hand in the original manuscript. Only a small portion is written in Carrie's hand, although she would take dictation more frequently in the future whenever needed. Wilkie also wrote many of the later instalments from his bed, but his immobility did not at all slow the pace of the book's events.

Indisputably identifying a true 'first' in the history of English letters is a nearly impossible feat that not only requires remarkable confidence in the scope of one's reading but also demands solid conviction that all relevant texts in a particular category have survived and been discovered. Nevertheless, T.S. Eliot famously declared in 'Wilkie Collins and Dickens' (published in *The Times Literary Supplement* on 4th August 1927) that *The Moonstone* was 'the first and greatest of English detective novels', carefully distinguishing the detective novel from the detective story, whose innovation he credited to Edgar Allan Poe. Detective figures and a focus on the resolution of a mystery turn up in novels that predate *The Moonstone*, and some of them merit consideration for the 'first' designation. Perhaps it is more useful to discuss *The Moonstone* as the detective novel whose plot devices, characterisation, and narrative method would become standards for the form and as the first to have achieved such instant and widespread fame. As with sensation fiction and most sub-genres of the novel, early mystery and detective novels drew from and overlapped with several existing genres, including the Gothic, sensationalism and psychological realism. In *The Moonstone*, for instance, Collins borrows details from an 1860 murder case in the village of Road in which a stained nightgown was a key piece of evidence against Constance Kent. The novel's plot twists are surprising but often so plausible that they do not feel as 'sensational' as the shocking developments in many of Collins' other novels. As Collins' writing emerged in the detective and mystery form, surprising elements became clues, not simply shock tactics. The revelation of those clues ultimately had much more to do with characters or readers overlooking something than with Collins attempting to produce gratuitous surprise.

Presented with the enormous Indian diamond of the novel's title at her eighteenth birthday dinner, Rachel Verinder notifies the household the next morning that the Moonstone has gone missing from her bedroom. The securely locked house has recently been visited by three Indians, who join the list of suspects alongside the Verinder family, their servants, and a set of overnight guests including two of Rachel's admirers (her cousins

Godfrey Ablewhite and Franklin Blake). Quickly, the servants become the prime targets of investigation, particularly Rosanna Spearman, a reformed thief with a deformed shoulder. Sergeant Cuff, a detective with a penchant for roses, makes headway in the case, but it is Ezra Jennings, the mysterious assistant of a local doctor, who devises an experiment that fully explains the crime.

Improving upon the narrative method of *The Woman in White*, Collins again structures the novel as a sequence of documents, this time using Franklin Blake as the presenter of testimonies from a wide range of characters. Each person can only speak about things they observe or events in which they participate directly, a structure that masterfully builds suspense and prevents any single narrator from revealing things they learn later. Gabriel Betteredge, the house steward who catches 'detective fever', is the novel's first narrator and one of Collins' most memorable. Betteredge's comical qualities, for instance his obsessive belief that the answers to all things in life lie within the pages of *Robinson Crusoe*, also connect to the novel's engagement with questions of empire (*Crusoe* is quite the coloniser) and dogmatic thinking. The next narrator, Miss Clack, is mercilessly satirised for proselytising not with *Crusoe* but with evangelical tracts. In the homes and amongst the linens of unsuspecting acquaintances, she deposits small books, particularly after failed attempts to guide conversations towards readings from her favourite instructional chapters, such as 'Satan in the Hair Brush' or 'Satan Under the Tea Table'. Some of the brilliance of Collins' writing lies in the abruptness of the transition from Betteredge to Clack. No stylistic quirks or syntactical habits remind the reader of Betteredge, and throughout the novel, each new narrator speaks in a fresh voice. That Collins holds the pen behind them all stands as a testament to his storytelling greatness.

The narrators by no means encompass all of the novel's intriguing characters, many of whom are sympathetic misfit figures. Rosanna Spearman merits pity not only because of her troubled past and deformity but also because most of her peers and superiors deny her even the possibility of having romantic feelings. The novel presents Franklin Blake's obliviousness to the potential that a servant could love him as a cause for censure, and Spearman's voice, presented in the form of a letter once she no longer resides in the Verinder household, is a more direct narrative voice than Rachel Verinder ever possesses. *The Moonstone* also shows Collins extending his explorations of homoerotic relationships between women. 'Limping' Lucy Yolland articulates a deep love for Rosanna and a vision of the women living 'like sisters' that offers a safer future for Rosanna than the one that follows her spontaneous desire for Blake (First Period, Ch XXIII). Ezra Jennings, whose past also involves heartbreak, is the novel's most captivating misfit. With piebald black and white hair loudly signalling his racial mixture, a 'gipsy' complexion, and an addiction to opium for pain relief, Jennings not only saves the life of the doctor who employs him but also deciphers the doctor's fever-deranged mumblings to enable the novel's resolution. Together, these outcasts possess the crucial information upon which the plot relies, yet they remain tragically expendable.

The trio of Indian brahmins charged with protecting the Moonstone first appears in the novel's opening document, which takes readers back to the storming of Seringapatam in 1799. Tracing the diamond's origin back even further, Collins embeds the contemporary 'adventures' of the diamond in imperial violence, suggesting that the current generation of brahmins have a more legitimate right to the diamond than those who have inherited it as a result of the plunder of British invaders: specifically, Rachel Verinder's uncle, John Herncastle. By returning readers to India at the novel's conclusion and showing an Orientalised but solemn and respectful view of Hindu religious ceremonies, *The Moonstone* builds upon the sentiment Collins expressed in 'A Sermon for Sepoys' and shows that, ten years after the Indian Rebellion, he remained invested in countering images of Indians as irrationally savage.

The launch of *The Moonstone* in 1868 was smooth, and by the end of its run, Collins' readers queued up outside the *All the Year Round* offices in anticipation of the diamond's final whereabouts. Collins, though, was not able to give himself over to carefree enjoyment of the novel's progression. On top of his illness, domestic disruptions distracted him. Sometime in the spring of 1868, his relationship with Caroline began to falter. There is no way to know how long tension may have been brewing, or which events were catalysts for others, but by the summer, Caroline had moved out of the lodgings at Gloucester Place. In the autumn, she married another man. Over the same span of time, Wilkie had set up another lover, Martha Rudd, in quarters on Bolsover Street.

These developments, however, do not come together to form a simple narrative of lovers finding new partners and separating. In these years, Collins' romantic and sexual arrangements became more unconventional than ever. The most likely scenario that explains Collins taking Rudd as a lover is that he met her on the trip he had taken with Pigott and Ward to investigate scenes for *Armadale*. Martha worked as an inn servant in the area of Great Yarmouth, where Wilkie stayed. This meeting would have taken place in the summer of 1864, and in December of that year, when Wilkie and Caroline moved house, Caroline stopped using the name she had adopted in 1860, 'Mrs Collins', in favour of Graves. The forty-year-old Wilkie's liaison with the nineteen-year-old Martha may have stirred Caroline's desire to jettison the wifely alias. On her part, Caroline had commenced some sort of relationship with a man approximately ten years her junior. Joseph Clow, age twenty-seven, came from a financially comfortable family of distillers, and on 29th October 1868, Caroline married him. Wilkie – in a gesture that could have signalled anything from defiance to well-wishing – attended the ceremony with Carrie and Dr Beard.

After Caroline's departure, Wilkie did not move Martha into Gloucester Place or move himself permanently into Bolsover

Street, about nine blocks away. Rather, he maintained Gloucester Place without Caroline in it and spent time with Martha separately. When he visited Bolsover Street, he was welcomed as Mr Dawson, a barrister, and Martha assumed the identity of his wife, Mrs Dawson. Possibly the most unusual aspect of the whole affair is not that Carrie stayed with Collins, working as his secretary, but that Carrie's grandmother also remained at Gloucester Place. One would not necessarily expect Collins' adopted daughter, now age seventeen, to move into Clow's home. It is far more surprising for the exiting partner's mother-in-law from a previous marriage to remain in the household. Mrs Graves' continued residency at Gloucester Place is further evidence that Wilkie bore Caroline no ill will and that his love for Martha did not interfere with the bonds of the extended family he had pieced together with Caroline.

That Collins ushered Caroline out of one home, set up Martha in another, and took loads of opium while he was penning *The Moonstone*, which vies with *The Woman in White* for status as his best novel, shows the depth of his strength – and I daresay virility – even in the midst of severe physical illness. The booming sales of the novels in the 1860s provided the financial security he needed to continue courting women and living the indulgent lifestyle he loved with little anxiety.

Theatricalities

At Bolsover Street, Martha Rudd immediately became pregnant. The approaching increase in responsibility may have provided extra motivation for the 45-year-old Collins to try quitting opium again early in 1869. This time, injections of morphine replaced laudanum for a short time. The stresses of impending father-hood, adjusting to life without Caroline, and attempting to decrease his opium use did not stop Collins from writing. His difficulty navigating major life changes, however, seems to have contributed to him spending a noticeably large amount of his time with Fred and Nina Lehmann rather than with Martha at Bolsover Street or with Carrie at Gloucester Place in the year 1869. Wilkie had been acting as Carrie's father since she was small, and Martha, aged twenty-four, bore him his first known biological child, Marian, on 4th July 1869. (One has to wonder if Collins' repeated licentious outings on the Continent had pro-duced pregnancies of which he never learned.) Wilkie was care-ful to make sure that Martha was taken care of, but, like many Victorian fathers, he was perfectly content to be away from Bolsover Street for the most trying weeks of a newborn's life. For the summer of 1869, he regularly stayed at Highgate with the Lehmanns, writing his next novel. Collins called Martha and Marian his 'morganatic family', a complicated choice of words since 'morganatic' refers to the spouse of lower rank in a socially unequal marriage who may not inherit the wealthier partner's fortune or title. Collins used the term frequently in his letters, but he also foiled its consequences by providing for Martha in his will. With the married fake identities of Mr and Mrs Dawson, Collins also ensured that the public face of Martha and the children was socially sanctioned. His biological children did not meet the world as 'illegitimate' or fatherless offspring; they shared Collins' assumed name, and their mother was settled in a comfortable home as a wife.

It is fitting that Collins' personal life was full of performance, given his longstanding interest in theatre. Due to the state of copyright laws, the subject of much complaint from Collins, Dickens, and others, Collins would sometimes immediately publish a dramatised version of his work in order to secure his own copyright over the play before others could rush adaptations to the stage. Increasingly, Collins wrote original dramas or simultaneously composed a dramatic and novelistic version of a story. A writer of sensation fiction, Collins was already comfortable with and well-versed in the similar plot conventions of melodrama. Impersonation, crime, and feminine virtue in jeopardy figure heavily in both genres, as do shocking revelatory scenes and hyperbolic emotion. In the 'Dedication' for an 1862 edition of *Basil*, Collins himself called novels and plays 'twin-sisters' and explained 'that the one is a drama narrated, as the other is a drama acted; and that all the strong and deep emotions which the Play-writer is privileged to excite, the Novel-writer is privileged to excite also'. Still, important factors prevent conflation of the two genres. Sensation fiction often profoundly blurs the stark good versus evil dichotomy of melodrama. Characters, such as Lydia Gwilt, who are conflicted about their murderous deeds or who believe themselves to be struggling against the worst sides of their own natures populate Collins' fiction and force a complicated evaluation of how good and evil are defined, experienced, and understood. Because his sensation fiction features so much ambiguity, some of Collins' turns to more simplified melodrama are surprising.

Following *The Moonstone*, *Black and White* feels jarringly melo-dramatic even though it shows the development of themes and concerns Collins had begun to explore in his fiction. The idea for the first two acts of the play came from Charles Fechter, with whom Collins shared authorial credit on the title page. Collins composed the dialogue and worked out the ending. *Black and White*, as its title suggests, deals with the dangers facing those of mixed racial origins. Set in Trinidad on the first day of the year 1830, the play immediately creates high melodrama and intrigue among Miss Emily Milburn and her rival lovers. Miss Milburn has fallen in love with Count Maurice de Leyrac on a trip to Paris, and her spurned fiancé, Stephen Westcraft, villainously takes advantage of the revelation that Leyrac is technically a slave. On her deathbed, Leyrac's mother (a 'quadroon' who has only then revealed her true identity) explains that Leyrac is her son by her former master. Adopted by a count and countess who conceal his origins, Leyrac has the legal standing of a slave on Trinidadian soil.

Rousing opposition to slavery by showing how people under-stood to be 'white' may be affected by the institution rather than exposing the horrors experienced by those whose visible skin colour condemns them to suffer, the play is not noteworthy for the particulars of its abolitionist stance. Collins depicts the slaves and their dialect as offensively simple and calls the group agit-ating for freedom 'the Thickskull Club'. Miss Milburn's shift from horror that 'A slave's *lips* have touched mine!' to her public avowal of love for that slave as well as the reversal of power between Leyrac and his servant David are far more interesting elements. David, for instance, turns out to be Leyrac's owner for a time, and when he discovers the document that frees Leyrac, he welcomes the 'chance to serve my slave'. Collins complained that the play's poor reception was due to audience fatigue with the topic of slavery because Harriet Beecher Stowe's *Uncle Tom's Cabin* had been dramatised in England so frequently. Even with Charles Fechter in the starring role when the show opened on

29th March 1869, four years after the conclusion of the American Civil War, the Adelphi Theatre was often empty during its two-month run, and Collins lost money.

His next work, *Man and Wife*, first appeared as a novel, but its original conception as a play is evident in highly charged face-offs and passages that sound like stage directions, such as: 'she threw herself theatrically on her knees before Julius' (Ch XLV). Some paragraphs even acknowledge a lack of natural description, which, given the novel's slow pacing and length, would probably have added a necessary depth to its subject. *Man and Wife* combined a tested theme, the absurdities of inconsistent marriage laws across the United Kingdom, with a new one, the absurdities of excessive athleticism in the education of young men. The plot turns on confusion resulting from the same Scottish statute that had humorously benefited the hero of *A Rogue's Life*: the law established a man and woman as married simply because the couple said as much publicly or in writing. The rogue of *Man and Wife*, Geoffrey Delamyn, reluctantly agrees to use these means to marry Anne Silvester, whom he has impregnated, but the plan turns into a hopelessly complicated legal and romantic mess. When Delamyn sends his friend, Arnold Brinkworth, to meet Silvester at an inn with a message explaining his delay, Brinkworth (in love with Blanche, whom Anne regards as a sister) must present himself as Silvester's husband to avoid offending the landlady. A storm forces them to pass the night together in a suite of rooms, which allows Delamyn to later claim that Brinkworth is Silvester's legal husband until Delamyn's own letter to Silvester proves that she is Delamyn's wife.

The novel's outrage at the legalised disempowerment of married women struck a familiar chord to readers of sensation fiction and affirmed the concerns of those advocating the Married Women's Property Act, passed at the end of the book's serialisation in 1870. Hester Dethridge, a cook who chooses to fall mute after a blow to the head from her spouse causes a speech impediment, repeatedly seeks help from the law to prevent her drunken husband from stealing her wages, selling her household furniture and beating her. The blame for her resorting to murder plainly lies with society at large, as does culpability for Anne Silvester's fear of marital rape and near murder at the hands of Geoffrey Delamyn. The novel's underlying critique, then, aims at extremist behaviour. Hester illustrates that a prime danger of inequitable marriage laws is that habitual oppression over lengthy periods of time turns battered or abused individuals into pathological killers; for, after she kills her brutal husband, her homicidal urges do not cease. In the case of Delamyn, his obsession with individual advancement is an extreme form of social ambition that leads to equally murderous derangement. Delamyn's manipulative imprisonment of Anne in the culminating scenes harks back to Laura Fairlie's incarceration in *The Woman in White* as well as to the Gothic tropes, including murderous contraptions between bedrooms, of Collins' early stories.

Collins' first novel to follow *The Moonstone*, *Man and Wife* appears in retrospect as a sort of bridge piece that moves from nuanced studies of character and circumstance to explorations that focus on jarring extremes, consistent with more of an emphasis on melodrama. The book also begins a thread of increasingly essentialist statements about sexual hierarchy that run inconsistently through Collins' later works. Reflecting upon a heretofore independent widow's attraction to Geoffrey Delamyn's domineering conduct and physical prowess (promptly showcased in the 'lithe and supple loins' revealed by his tight running costume), the narrator declares:

> … the natural condition of a woman is to find her master in a man. Look in the face of any woman who is in no direct way dependent on a man – and, as certainly as you see the sun in a cloudless sky, you see a woman who is not happy. The want of a master is their great unknown want; the

possession of a master is – unconsciously to themselves – the only possible completion of their lives. (Ch XXXV)

The tone of such statements is less jocular and more rigid than Collins' earlier works, in which Ezra Jennings, for instance, has a 'female constitution' and Rachel Verinder has masculine qualities. Readers continue to debate whether transgressive heroines who marry in Victorian fiction are ultimately 'tamed' by the institution, and Collins' later novels provide ample fodder for such deliberations. Similarly, *Man and Wife* also shows Collins developing a familiar theme, evident especially in *Armadale*, that reappears in works such as *The Legacy of Cain*: whether or not present generations are fated to repeat the past. The notion of doubling via descent presents itself in Blanche and Anne, carbon copies of their mothers in personal disposition as well as devotion to one another. The late fiction continues to ponder questions of hereditary character traits and hereditary 'doom', resisting a uniform answer.

Although the story increased the circulation of *Cassell's Magazine*, Collins' relationship with the editors was not free from tension. His response to their complaints about some profanity in the early weekly instalments provides a clear articulation of Collins' views on censorship. Having eliminated a 'damn', he warned against considering such deletions as a precedent:

Readers who object to expletives in books, are – as to my experience – readers who object to a great many other things in books, which they are too stupid to understand. It is quite possible that your peculiar constituency may take exception to things to come in my story, which are essential to the development of character, or which are connected with a much higher and larger moral point of view than they are capable of taking themselves.

– 25th September 1869

Readers, stupid or otherwise, loved the novel and seemed to have no trouble comprehending Collins' points. *Cassell's* published instalments from November of 1869 to July of 1870, and the first three-volume edition sold out even before the final serial had appeared.

Man and Wife's completion coincided with great sadness for Collins: the death of Charles Dickens on 9th June 1870. Although Dickens' health had been weakening for some time, his determination to continue walking long distances, giving public readings, and writing for several hours per day indicated that he was in no way accepting imminent death. His closest acquaintances were stunned at the passing of a personal friend as well as an icon of the age. Wilkie and Charley Collins both attended the funeral, and Wilkie remained tremendously saddened by the loss. Several years later, he reflected on the relationship in correspondence with an early Dickens biographer, Robert du Pontavice de Heussey. In a letter of 15th March 1886, referring to the 1855 Paris trip, Collins recalled, 'We saw each other every day, and were as fond of each other as men could be.'

While he was mourning his friend of nearly twenty years, the other central friendship in Collins' life rebounded surprisingly. At some point in late 1870 or early 1871, Caroline Graves returned to Gloucester Place. Her marriage to Joseph Clow, for reasons that remain mysterious, failed, and she resumed her life with Wilkie. Dickens had speculated in a letter to his sister-in-law that Caroline married out of spite, giving Wilkie an ultimatum to try to force him into marriage when he was taking up with Martha Rudd.[8] It is, of course, possible that Caroline desired a marriage with Wilkie. There are several good reasons, however, to pause at Dickens' (and some of Collins' biographers') speculations. If Caroline had threatened Wilkie, and he called her bluff, it is questionable whether a strong-willed woman who had survived independently years earlier would have gone through with an insincere marriage ceremony for the sake of pride. Moreover, after so many years of living together unmarried, it would seem likely that the couple had a solid understanding of one another's views on the subject. Collins' surviving letters refer to Caroline as a constant companion, not a nagging, impatient-for-marriage lover. By the early springtime of 1871, she was comfortably back in the household and part of a life that now included Martha and her children.

Ironically, Wilkie taking a second mistress placed Caroline in a more wifely role. Caroline went out publicly with Wilkie to the theatre or to dinners with friends, and they travelled together, whereas Martha remained at home. Wilkie and Martha's second child, Harriet Constance, was born on 14th May 1871, coinciding closely with the time of Caroline's return. Now, Wilkie's mother, biological daughter, and adopted daughter (plus her grandmother) were all named Harriet. Martha's children would sometimes spend holidays with Caroline and Wilkie, but Caroline and Martha did not keep company. Collins took his responsibilities to Martha and her children no less seriously than a good husband would. As he had done for Marian, Collins immediately added Harriet Constance to his last will and testament.

Instead of immediately capitalising on the popularity of *Man and Wife* with a dramatisation, Collins decided to adapt his first blockbuster novel for the stage. He radically changed *The Woman in White*, adding scenes and fundamentally altering the timing of the plot. The villain, Count Fosco, became the most crucial role. Wisely, since so many viewers already knew the plot of the novel, Collins focused the play not on moments of shocking revelation but on the audience's superior awareness of the fullness of the characters' situations. This development of dramatic irony avoided some of the excesses expected of melodrama and served Collins well. After months of draining preparation and rehearsal, the play opened spectacularly on 9th October 1871 at the Olympic Theatre. Reviewers and general audiences alike were impressed, and subsequent performances continued to sell out. *The Woman in White* enjoyed a run of over four months at the Olympic then a tour for which Collins further changed the script, primarily to shorten the four-hour-long running time. Following such a triumph, *Man and Wife* finally opened on 22nd February 1873 to great anticipation. The show was an enormous hit at the Prince of Wales Theatre, where the Prince himself saw it multiple times. It lasted over five months then had a long touring life, securing Collins' place as a well-respected English dramatist. The excitement attending the production was also due to the advancements it helped bring to the Victorian stage. Some of the special effects, such as electric lighting, were technologies appearing for the first time in an English theatre. *The Woman in White*, by contrast, had used simple sets.

As Collins' enjoyment of *Man and Wife*'s success in novel form had been hampered by Dickens' death, another great loss dimmed the play's debut. On 9th April 1873, Charles Allston Collins succumbed to the stomach cancer that had ailed him for so long. His marriage to Kate may not have been passionate, but she nursed him carefully at the end of his life. William Holman Hunt, one of the founders of the Pre-Raphaelite Brotherhood to which Charley never fully belonged, drew a touching 'Deathbed Portrait'. In the corner appears a tribute to Charles' own creative work: an excerpt from his 1859 book, *A New Sentimental Journey*. The passage states that it is a comfort to think of surviving loved ones visiting graves so as not to forget the departed. It is worth noting, however, that Hunt excised a substantial portion of text in his tribute, eliminating Collins' detailed rendering of corpses rotting underground in order to maintain the deathbed sketch's consoling tone. Although Charles Collins never prevailed over the crises of confidence that ended his painting career, he remained a productive author, having published a substantial amount of periodical writing and three novels – *Straithcairn* (1864), *The Bar Sinister* (1864), and *At the Bar* (1866) – at the time of his death. Wilkie was with Charley at the end to witness his relief from suffering, but he had surely expected to see his younger brother live past the age of forty-five. In a far different place as a writer and as a man since he wrote their father's biography, Wilkie composed the *Dictionary of National Biography* entry for Charley.

Just over a month after Charley's death and only three months after *Man and Wife* opened, *The New Magdalen* debuted at the Olympic Theatre on 19th May 1873. Collins was keeping himself excessively busy with playwriting, which had the benefit of providing respite from his grief. He wrote to George Bentley, 'Happily for <u>me</u> – after the loss that I have sustained – I have had hardly a moment to myself since the miserable day that my brother died' (8th May 1873). *The New Magdalen*, published in *Temple Bar* from October of 1872 to July of 1873, was simultaneously before the public in multiple forms. One could purchase volume editions of the novel or see it performed as a play before the instalments in *Temple Bar* had concluded.

The story's heroine, Mercy Merrick, is a fallen woman through no fault of her own. Having survived a childhood of extreme poverty and neglect, the young Mercy finds employment as a servant with a generous couple whom she comes to regard as adopted parents. When the husband takes liberties and tries to seduce the naive girl as an adolescent, she flees from the house in horror. Existing scantly on needlework, Mercy is the victim of an appalling rape after she collapses from exhaustion on the street. She wakes in a brothel surrounded by unsympathetic prostitutes, remembers a man giving her wine to drink, and realises that she was violated while drugged. The revelation of her past thwarts Mercy's multiple and genuine attempts to break away from her street life until she escapes by working as a nurse in the Franco-Prussian War. Mercy returns to England under the stolen identity of Grace Roseberry, a colleague Mercy believes to have died during a shelling. When Grace returns to England and tries to reclaim her identity, *The New Magdalen* inverts the core of *The Woman in White* by emphasising a complete lack of female solidarity. Grace barely sympathises with Mercy before the shelling and becomes even more repellent when she (understandably) tries to expose Mercy's scheme. It is the threat of seeing Grace incarcerated in a madhouse that finally leads Mercy to confess, at which point her fiancé breaks their engagement.

Because of its conclusion, when Collins staged *The New Magdalen*, he broke through social restraints even more radically than he had done with the publication of his novels. One of the main characters, Reverend Julian Gray, is a clergyman, and presenting clergymen onstage was only minimally tolerated. On top of that, this particular preacher finds happiness by marrying Mercy in place of the cowardly fiancé. Although the clergy may have been perfectly righteous as rehabilitators of prostitutes, the suggestion that they might lust after such women was more than alarming to the status quo and raised uncomfortable questions about presumably saintly reformatory methods. The serial of the story had found a warm reception, but book sales were disappointing, and Collins blamed Charles Mudie's monopolistic circulating library. Mudie had wanted Collins to change the provocative title, a request at which Collins scoffed. Given its scandalous components, the play's unqualified success was surprising. Its continued staging in England, the United States (where sales of the book had been strong) and on the Continent did draw criticism from those who found its moral position to be unacceptably relaxed, but such complaints did nothing to diminish audiences. Ada Cavendish, also the play's producer, impressed Collins in the role of Mercy Merrick, and the two remained good friends.

Throughout these theatrical productions, Collins also kept up his non-dramatic fiction writing. In 1871, he wrote *Miss or Mrs?* for the Christmas number of *The Graphic*. Calling to mind Collins' love of sailing, *Miss or Mrs?* introduces its characters on a yacht where Mr Launcelot Linzie jumps from the bulwark to extol the virtues of bathing naked in the sea. Told in twelve fast-paced 'Scenes', the novella is the story of Natalie Graybrooke, who loves her cousin Launcelot but is betrothed by her father, Sir Joseph, to Richard Turlington, the yacht's 'swarthy' owner.

Collins admirably captures the interpersonal tensions that accompany sea life and the urgency of stolen private moments between lovers in such confined spaces. The couple's saga involves classic sensation techniques – spying servants, secret ceremonies, and attempted murder – but the sudden shooting off of someone's face makes the novella's concluding events considerably more grisly than most.

Natalie Graybrooke's beauty and sexual maturity are attributed to her deceased mother, a woman with 'a mixture of Negro blood and French blood' from Martinique. At five feet seven inches tall, Natalie's proportions are 'Amazonian' and her skin tone a complimentary 'warm dusky colour' (First Scene). Here and elsewhere, including the brief appearance of a 'mulatto' lawyer in *Man and Wife*, Collins shows that mixture permeates English society, suffusing the circles in which the gentry move. The story's sympathies lie with Natalie's marriage to Launce, and her racial mixture never surfaces as a source of danger. In fact, Sir Joseph's markedly English personality traits are far more harmful than Natalie's, and his refusal to see anything other than money-making potential in Richard Turlington is even more frightening than Turlington's near inability to conceal his cruel nature. Sir Joseph refuses to take Natalie's objections to the marriage seriously, caring only about Turlington's ability to help the family make more money and believing that Natalie will grow into love: 'So the average ignorance of human nature, and the average belief in conventional sentiment, complacently contemplated the sacrifice of one more victim on the all-devouring altar of Marriage!' (Fourth Scene). Collins leaves his readers wondering whether any couple can truly be happy at the altar of an 'all-devouring' institution.

Poor Miss Finch deals with colour a bit differently, featuring a blue character. With a plot that now strikes one as downright hilarious, familiar sensation hallmarks appear in abundance. Lucilla Finch, who is blind and afraid of dark colours, falls in love with a man who develops epilepsy after a brutal robbery attack, and the silver nitrate he must use to cure his epilepsy turns his skin blue. Lucilla does not know that her beloved, Oscar Dubourg, is blue when her eyesight is restored, so she is easily fooled by his identical twin, Nugent, who impersonates Oscar and tries to marry her. Poor Miss Finch indeed. Luckily for her, Oscar thwarts his nefarious twin (who eventually freezes to death on an Arctic expedition), and the effects of the medical procedure dwindle so that she is once again blind when reunited with Oscar, whose blueness she can blissfully ignore.

The novel also speaks to the issue of colour difference as it pertains to ethnicity rather than colour-altering medications. Lucilla irrationally fears a 'Hindoo' at her aunt's home and sees nothing but 'brown demons' and 'black-eyed beings' when she thinks of the man, even having to leave the table when seated next to him (Ch XX). Her aunt, Miss Batchford, prizes social respectability and is offended by Lucilla's behaviour. The novel stresses the unreasonable nature of Lucilla's feelings, and she defends them by explaining that she cannot change her train of thought because she is unable to see for herself that the dark people are harmless. She astutely faults people who can see for their fears because they have the ability to visually witness the harmlessness of the subjects of their phobias, yet their fears persist. The extremity of the novel's examples undercuts what is actually a fairly sophisticated commentary on human perceptions of colour difference and the sheer stupidity of racist thinking.

Unlike much of Collins' later fiction, *Poor Miss Finch* was not written for the stage, and Collins develops an excellent narrator in Mrs Pratolungo, Lucilla's attendant. A self-described 'curious foreign woman' holding revolutionary and socialist views, Mrs Pratolungo simultaneously serves as a target for the novel's ridicule and as its most credible source of information. In her voice, the book includes marvellously funny moments, such as the following declaration of narrative authority: 'I happen to be one of the few people who can read dogs' language as written in dogs' faces. I correctly report the language of the gentleman sheep-dog on this occasion' (Ch II). Collins also retains his penchant for jolting readers with references to women's bodies, showing no regard for Victorian proprieties. Mrs Finch has fourteen children – a less than subtle satire of the reverend's sexual appetite – and always appears with a suckling infant and a novel in her arms. During one particularly uncomfortable domestic silence, Mrs Pratolungo reports, 'we can hear the baby sucking' (Ch XXIII). In these ways, Collins uses Mrs Pratolungo to achieve remarkable comic effect, but her narrative also contains powerful moments of suspense. The revelation of Oscar's attack, for instance, involves the horrific discovery of Jinks, a perfectly drawn three-year-old girl, with a haunting message written on the back of her frock in human blood.

At its best, *Poor Miss Finch* offers astute reflection on what it means to experience the world without sight. Collins carefully explores the limits but also the reaches of human sensory perception in his characterisation of Lucilla Finch, drawing upon sound medical sources such as William Cheselden's famous 1728 account of restoring sight to a thirteen-year-old boy. Regardless of Collins' careful research, critics disliked the novel exceedingly and were unsparing in reviews following its appearance in book form in January of 1872 (it had appeared in *Cassell's Magazine* from September of 1871 to February of 1872).

With more consistent enthusiasm greeting his books and plays in the United States, Collins followed through on his plans to visit the land. A seasoned visitor to Europe, on 13th September 1873, Collins set sail for a country he had never seen. He loved it. On his first night in the United States, he stayed in the very same room Dickens had occupied at the Westminster Hotel in New York. Collins, though flattered, was overwhelmed and fatigued by constant attention from the press and the public's insatiable appetite for sightings and autographs. He nevertheless appreciated the frankness of the American people and the opportunity to meet notable American figures, including Oliver Wendell Holmes, Mark Twain, and Napoleon Sarony, a distinguished photographer with whom he became friends. Without Caroline's or Martha's company, one also wonders what sorts of American women Wilkie might have met. During the trip, he was further pleased to see both *The New Magdalen* and *The Woman in White* open on Broadway. *The New Magdalen* was the more successful production, and, as in England, the initial run was followed by a long tour.

Charles Fechter, who had relocated to the United States, greeted Collins in New York and later hosted him at a farm in Pennsylvania, where Collins prepared for the reading tour. With an immensely profitable tour of the United States in 1867, Dickens had established a new precedent for authors wishing to charge fees for public readings, laying to rest the fear that such a mercenary endeavour would sully novelists' reputations. Collins lengthened 'The Dream Woman', which had appeared as 'The Ostler' in the 1855 Christmas number *The Holly Tree Inn* then later in *The Queen of Hearts*, and worked up selections from *The Frozen Deep* for his readings. *The New York Times* reflected upon Collins and the tour in complimentary terms in its obituary: 'Personally he was an attractive character, and he had warm friends. His round, ruddy face, with beard and spectacles, and his slight, round-shouldered figure, gave him a somewhat professional look when in this country last. He read selections from his own works well, and made an excellent impression' (24th September 1889).

Thrilling to Wilkie was the fact that his health remained so strong during the trip. He attributed the gout's absence to the dry winter air, and his spirits soared even when he was uncomfortable on long railway journeys. In the course of doing some Canadian readings, he was unhampered by increased humidity around Niagara Falls, and the natural wonder of the place predictably amazed him. After visting many cities, including Chicago and Detroit, he had to end the trip slightly earlier than anticipated in order to help Martha Rudd move house. Collins departed Boston on 7th March for a warm greeting back in England from Martha, as evidenced by her promptly becoming pregnant with their third child.

The unconventionality of Collins' personal life was more than matched by the unusual features of his next fictional work. In *The Law and the Lady*, Collins fully indulged the shock qualities of sensation fiction, returning to some of the most explicit aspects of early works, such as *Basil*. *The Law and the Lady* follows Valeria Macallan's quest to eradicate an erroneous blight on her new husband's name. After discovering that Eustace Macallan has married her under a false name to conceal that he has been tried for the murder of his first wife, Valeria dedicates her life to clearing him of the suspicion that attaches itself to the Scottish verdict of 'Not Proven'. Eustace deserts Valeria, convinced that damning pieces of evidence will prevent her from ever being able to view him without scandalous ambiguity. With the dubious merit of being able to accurately spot true friends, a shared instinct among 'women, children and dogs', Valeria unconditionally believes in Eustace's innocence (Ch VIII). One of the very first novelistic women in a detective role, she persists in investigating the case, reviewing evidence, conducting interviews, and enlisting the help of many male acquaintances to vindicate her husband.

Although Collins' novel has recognisable similarities to Dickens' *Our Mutual Friend* (1864–5), which features a dust heap containing an important plot secret, and Charley Collins' *At the Bar* (1866), which includes a character accused of murdering a suicidal woman, *The Law and the Lady* certainly distinguishes itself with Miserrimus Dexter, Valeria's leg-free nemesis. One of Collins' most fascinating creations, the novel paints Dexter as a 'crack-brained personage' who is best understood as 'a mixture of the tiger and the monkey' (Ch XXII). Leaving his wheelchair to hurdle about on his hands, cooking truffles in a miniature kitchen, and flinging himself onto Valeria's lap in a fit of passion, Dexter is eccentric in the extreme. His rationality and manipulation obscure the true cause of the first Mrs Macallan's death, and it is only after Valeria pressures him into unintentionally revealing a crucial clue that Dexter's 'latent insanity' fully surfaces, leading to his death in a madhouse. Valeria routinely expresses sympathy for this man with no legs, but the novel is ulti-mately far less sympathetic to its disabled characters than Collins' earlier fiction. The implicit claim that the disabilities or deform-ities of Rosanna Spearman in *The Moonstone* and Madonna Grice in *Hide and Seek*, for instance, should not cause one to regard the characters as inferior or morally flawed is an argument missing from *The Law and the Lady*. Miserrimus Dexter, with womanly hair and beauty as well as masculine sexual aggression, may con-fuse Victorian models of binary thinking, but he emerges repeat-edly and finally as a repellent, if pitiful, freak of nature.

The incompleteness of the novel's quasi-resolution unsettles one further. The full explanation of Mrs Macallan's death and Eustace's innocence is so damaging to Eustace's character that, following Valeria's advice, he chooses not to read the discovered letter that proves his innocence. Furthermore, no public clearing of his name is possible without degrading the memory of his first wife, so the decision about whether to publicise the letter is left to the Macallans' newborn son. Once he matures, should he wish to expose the letter in order to re-establish the honour of his own name, the young Macallan will have the power to do so. In this way, the novel sets up a tense dilemma for the first-born son, who will have to disgrace his father in order to dispel his own shame as the son of a man never found innocent of murder.

The Law and the Lady's weekly publication in *The Graphic* from September of 1874 to March of 1875 proved to be the most upsetting encounter with Victorian prudery and censorship that Collins had experienced yet. One of the most unexpectedly rad-ical facets of Collins' portrayal of Valeria Macallan is that she turns out to have pursued her investigation – including her encounters with Dexter as well as her travels to Scotland, Spain, England, then Paris – while pregnant. Valeria agrees to abandon her pursuits in part because of her condition, but her accom-plishments while pregnant are far more impressive than her husband's cowardly flight from the crisis and subsequent descent into illness. Valeria challenges notions of essentialised passive women then explains her behaviour and curiosity as a fault of womanhood, exemplifying the troublesome propensity of Collins' later works to endorse a more restrictive feminine identity. Still, Arthur Locker, *The Graphic*'s editor, found the story's treatment of Valeria more risqué than he had anticipated, and he unilaterally excised a passage that he deemed vulgar.

The offending passage in Chapter XXXV describes the seated Miserrimus Dexter kissing Valeria's hand then forcefully holding her standing figure by the waist while she tries to free herself, his head positioned at her midsection. Exactly where in her midsection Dexter's head would fall is impossible to determine, but Locker claimed that the episode 'described an attempted violation of the heroine by Dexter, & was, according to the unanimous opinion of the directors, myself, & other members of the establishment, unfit to appear in the pages of a family newspaper. I did not apply to the author to alter it, because I judged, from previous experience, that he would refuse to do so.' As this action violated the terms of Collins' contract, he was able to force Locker to restore the deletions, but Locker had further complaints and urged Collins to change his drawing of Valeria's pregnancy:

> … *there is a disagreeable flavour pervading the story generally. An example of this occurs in the part for the present week when Valeria discovers that she is with child. Ladies don't care to have such subjects paraded in novels, & moreover – according to the judgment of two married ladies, Valeria's discovery is rather improbable, for women find out that they are pregnant, long before the quickening of the child, by other symptoms, the principal of which is of course the cessation of the monthly courses.*[9]

Collins was confident enough in his superior knowledge of women's bodies and reading tastes to refuse Locker's suggested changes, which led *The Graphic* to a rare exercise of its editorial prerogative. The newspaper used its own pages to apologise to its readers for publishing the story. Collins was, of course, outraged, but had little recourse once the denunciation had been printed.

Collins may have had extra inspiration for his drawing of a pregnant protagonist and personal reasons for his conviction that Locker's version of how women experienced pregnancy was not the only plausible one. On 25th December 1874, Martha Rudd gave birth to Wilkie's only son, William Charles Collins Dawson. Wilkie loved Charley as dearly as he did all of his children, but even the celebration of his son's birthday failed to redeem the dreaded holiday or to eclipse what he continued to call 'the horrors of Christmas' (19th December 1885). In the space of five and a half years, Wilkie had fathered three children with Martha. At Gloucester Place, Carrie, now in her twenties, was a daughter as well as a secretary. Now a father of four with two longstanding partners, Collins entered his sixth decade surrounded by large, loving families. Those families helped to provide important sustenance as it became increasingly difficult for Collins to work through illness, especially when downturns such as the ones in the spring of 1875 and '76 included a diminishment of his eyesight.

Collins' dramatic writing in the early 1870s established him as a playwright whose works thrived on stages in England, Europe, and the United States. His next adaptations, based on two of his best novels, did not build so solidly on that reputation. Dramatising *Armadale* eleven years after its publication, Collins sacrificed most of the psychological complexity that distinguished the novel. Oddly, the play focused on Dr Downward, the unsubtly named abortionist, as its principal villain even though its title drew attention to Lydia Gwilt, the no longer murderous governess. After a test run of the show at the Alexandra Theatre in Liverpool in December of 1875, *Miss Gwilt* opened at the Globe Theatre in April of 1876. Regarded now as one of Collins' poorer adaptations, the show did well enough with Ada Cavendish in the lead role to run for three months.

A reworking of *The Moonstone* in September of 1877 at the Olympic was much worse. Eliminating many of the novel's central attributes, such as opium use, and key characters, including Rosanna Spearman and Ezra Jennings, the play bore little resemblance to its source material. It is even more difficult to believe that Collins erased the Indians, so central to the development of the plot and also to the novel's commentary on British imperialism, from the play. Condensing the action into the events of a single day at the Verinder home, the script disastrously emphasised comedy over all else. The show did not fold for two months, but reviews were terrible, and some cast members quit. It opened on 17th September, and Collins was on his way to Italy with Caroline by the end of that month.

Collins' fiction at the time had been faring somewhat better than the plays. Two works from this period, *The Two Destinies* and *The Haunted Hotel*, each depicting seemingly paranormal events, show the uneven quality of Collins' later work and remind us that a good piece often followed a bad one. In *The Two Destinies*, apparitions and telepathy guide the protagonist to his lost childhood love, but improbably extreme changes in their physical appearances prevent each from recognising the other. Hester Dethridge's murderous apparition and Geoffrey Delamyn's clairvoyant nightmares in *Man and Wife* point forward to such themes, but discoveries of bigamy and repeatedly interrupted suicides do not add much credibility to events already triggered by ghosts in *The Two Destinies*. Published in *Temple Bar* from January to September of 1876 with subsequently strong book sales, little recommends the novel to current readers, and some of Collins' contemporaries disparaged its absurdity. An unsigned piece in *The Saturday Review* on 20th January 1877 called it 'an amazingly silly book'.

The Haunted Hotel, on the other hand, provokes more thoughtful consideration of prophecies and departed spirits as the relatives of a murdered lord are unable to sleep, even unknowingly, in the chamber where he died. Killed by his wife and her mad scientist brother for an insurance policy benefit, Lord Montbarry leaves behind a murderous widow who now goes by countess Narona, among other names. Montbarry's jilted former fiancée, Agnes, mourns him deeply and gently puts off the advances of his brother, Henry. The intriguing countess is convinced that destiny will continue to unite her with Agnes and that Agnes' forgiving spirit will only lead to a dreadful series of events. The story never resolves the question of whether it is the countess' strong will to believe in a particular fate or fate itself that determines her end. Full of gory details, including an actual and reeking severed head, the tale is undoubtedly chilling. It is also salacious, implying incest between the countess and the man who either is, or poses as, her brother. Furthermore, when Agnes allows herself to contemplate Henry's attraction, she provokes the following suggestive warning: 'What lurking temptations to forbidden tenderness find their hiding-places in a woman's dressing-gown, when she is alone in her room at night!' (Ch XXII). Fruitlessly, Agnes tries to distract herself from fleshly desires with a book about Venice.

Published in *Belgravia* from June to November of 1878, *The Haunted Hotel* shows Collins mixing suspense, fear and fairly explicit sensuality with a bit of self-ridicule. In an apparent sendup of Collins' own melodramatic efforts, the countess frantically writes herself to death as she composes a confession in the form of a play. Few plays were left in Collins' pen, but many more novels were to come. Having lost his brother Charley and his friend Dickens, Wilkie was grateful that his surviving friends, children, and lovers were able to spend time with him as he continued to write, sometimes experimentally.

A Painful Decline

Inconsistency in the quality of Collins' literary work alongside a regrettable consistency in the poor state of his health characterised the final decade and a half of Collins' life. When the gout struck his eyes, even the temporary impossibility of continuing the activities at the core of his life, reading and writing, was miserable to endure. In a note of apology to a friend whose morning visit he missed because the previous restless night kept him in bed, Wilkie's frustration breaks through as he exclaims, 'No more of my infirm self!' (30th September 1886). Although he could not regularly visit friends as much as he would have liked, nor provide the splendid dinners he and Caroline had enjoyed hosting, Wilkie never succumbed to complete despondency. He enjoyed his families, kept his children close, wrote playful letters as often as he could, and refused to stop telling stories.

With *The Fallen Leaves*, published in various venues beginning with *The World* in January of 1879, Collins decided to see how the public reacted to what he called the 'First Series' before writing a planned sequel. He knew that his attempt to examine the hypocrisies of multiple societies by viewing the lives of downtrodden women from various perspectives would be controversial, but he was flat wrong in anticipating any kind of positive response. Reviewers as well as run-of-the-mill readers hated the book, and Collins abandoned all plans to continue the story of Amelius Goodhart, a Christian Socialist, and a feeble-minded former prostitute called 'Simple Sally'. Amelius must leave his life in the United States because, although his utopian community does not require marriage before sex, they do insist on elders approving each union, and Amelius participates in an unsanctioned one. Once in London, where he grows close to several women who turn out to be related, he rescues Sally from the street and eventually marries her. The idea that Collins' novel would advocate for the reform of prostitutes was not what primarily upset reviewers and readers. He had treated that subject before, and countless other writers had wondered what should be done with fallen women. It was the absurdity of the plot, which included baby theft as well as uncompelling characters, and the book's offensive amount of detail that left readers so hostile. This work, about societal attitudes towards unconventional marriage arrangements, is the one that Wilkie dedicated simply 'To Caroline'.

Just as *The Fallen Leaves* had begun its appearance in print, Edward (Ned) Ward, whose elopement Collins had helped arrange so many years ago, committed suicide by gruesomely cutting his own throat. It took five days for him to die, and the whole incident rattled Wilkie both as a friend and as godfather to Ward's eldest daughter, now thirty years old. Ward's surrender to depression deepened the sadness Wilkie felt when reminiscing about his younger days. On 16th January, one day after Ward's death, Collins began editing *A Rogue's Life* for republication. Its preface explains, 'The revising of these pages has been to me a melancholy task. I can only hope that they may cheer the sad moments of others.' Dreamed up in 1856 when he was in the midst of cavorting through the streets of Paris with Dickens and other now-deceased friends, the adventures of the rogue threw into vivid relief the condition of the 55-year-old Wilkie, who was too ill even to attend Ward's funeral.

Revisiting the past was beneficial when Collins focused on proven successes like *A Rogue's Life*, but embarrassments like *The Red Vial* would have been well enough left alone. Instead,

Collins turned the play that had irritated audiences in 1858 into *Jezebel's Daughter*, a novel serialised in multiple newspapers in 1880. On top of a plot that used poisoning, a reanimated corpse, then more poisoning, Collins added a widowed philanthropist, Mrs Wagner, who advocates for the ethical treatment of lunatics. Another widow, Madame Fontaine, learns about chemical mixtures from her husband and uses them to further financial and romantic designs. The concern with poisoning and antidotes both recalls *Armadale*'s Lydia Gwilt and anticipates *The Guilty River* but with far less effective characterisation. *Jezebel's Daughter*'s powerful descriptions of the abuses at Bedlam Hospital and its laudable plea for civil handling of the insane did little to rescue it, and Collins did better with the material that formed his next project, *The Black Robe*.

Published in *The Sheffield and Rotherham Independent* from October 1880 to March 1881 as well as in the United States and Canada, *The Black Robe* is often overlooked in appraisals of Collins' career that hastily dismiss all of his later fiction as meritless. Stella Eyrecourt, in name and marital prospects, recalls the heroine of Charlotte Brontë's famous 1847 novel. Unlike Jane Eyre, whose wedding is interrupted in the breath before the swearing of vows, Stella learns of her new husband's wife while exiting the nuptial church. And unlike Mr Rochester, who conceals the existence of his wife, Mr Winterfield truly believes his wife to be dead. Able to nullify the marriage immediately, Stella manages to escape public scandal, but after she marries Lewis Romayne (with whom she falls in love at first sight), the conniving of a Catholic priest who wishes to return the Romayne estate to the hands of the Church reveals her ill-fated first marriage ceremony. Recalling Father Rocco of 'The Yellow Mask', Father Benwell is unstoppable in his quest to repossess the former Abbey. He convinces Romayne that only marriages consecrated in a church are valid and that human law cannot sever such unions. Romayne therefore regards his recent bride Stella as the actual wife of Mr Winterfield and enters the priesthood. Winterfield, freed by his wife's actual death, finally persuades Stella to marry him. Ironically, then, the novel's favoured coupling is also the one that Benwell and the Church maliciously insist upon as true.

The well-executed battle between those wishing to convert Romayne to Catholicism and those wishing to see him married to Stella shows the liveliness of the best of Collins' earlier writing. That struggle also involves one of the most interesting homo-erotic relationships of Collins' novels. Arthur Penrose, whose name has seemingly endless phallic and romantic meanings, is the young priest Father Benwell hopes will convert Romayne. The novel places Penrose in direct competition with Stella for Romayne's affections even after Romayne and Stella marry. The title of one chapter puts the question explicitly: 'The Priest or the Woman?'. Romayne's chief deficiency of character is a 'coldness toward women', and his friend Lord Loring is confident that 'nothing of that sort is incurable, if we can only find the right woman' ('Before the Story', Ch X). Stella captures Romayne's attentions, but Penrose loves him with his 'whole heart', trembling and crying whenever they must endure long partings (Bk II, Ch IV). Penrose frequently calls Romayne his 'brother in love', which recalls Mr Winterfield's attempts to cloak his enduring romantic love for Stella by promising – with tongue firmly in cheek – to remain in the role of a 'brother' ('After the Story', Ch II). In part, the novel attempts to justify the homoeroticism by excluding women on essentialist grounds from the intellectualism that binds the men. Even stepping in as amanuensis, Stella can never hope to replicate the intimacy of men joined in true scholarly inquiry. The extent of the homoerotic bond between Penrose and Romayne exceeds the more critically commented upon pairing of Allan Armadale and Ozias Midwinter in *Armadale*. Yet there is no tainted family history to justify the parting of the pair in *The Black Robe*. Integrity lies at the core of the men's motives and feelings, and, even though the heterosexual pairing with Stella is the desired outcome that will thwart Benwell, Stella herself is won over by

Penrose. After risking death in an attempt to reach Romayne's deathbed, Penrose joins Stella as a guest at Winterfield's home.

One senses that Collins had fun writing this fast-paced novel. The book is full of amusing gems, including a revolutionary 'sandwich dance' and a housekeeper with the strongest of opinions on when to serve oyster omelettes. We find a touching reflection on the reunion of a dog with its owner after Winterfield has denied his dog the birthright indicated in its name, Traveller, by journeying abroad alone. Collins also sends some humorous respect in his father's direction when Romayne, admiring the 'matchless English landscape painters of half a century since', feels that he 'could kiss' a seascape (Bk III, Ch IV). The book deftly moves between a light-hearted third-person narrator and the presentation of documents or journal entries written by eyewitnesses. The testimonials recall the narrative structure that served Collins so well in *The Moonstone*, and the reappearance of the character of Mr Murthwaite makes plain that the novel was fresh in Collins' mind. *The Black Robe* also recalls several of Collins' earlier stories, particularly 'Mad Monkton', because both plots depict Catholic families and characters haunted by the consequences of duels abroad. 'Who Killed Zebedee?', published simultaneously with *The Black Robe* in December of 1880 and later as 'Mr Policeman and the Cook', also presents the deathbed confession of a Catholic policeman who leaves off prosecuting a murderer on account of his engagement to her.

Collins struggled to write much in the rough summer months of 1881 as severe gout attacks repeatedly disabled him. Even at Ramsgate, he was housebound, and the disorder in his eyes often prevented him from writing. Early in 1882, still severely disabled, he insisted on directing his creative energies into a new novel. *The Black Robe*'s hostile stance towards the Jesuits and its encouragement of theories that the Catholic Church was conspiring to take over England had drawn criticism. Partly in response to those complaints, Collins imagined a Catholic heroine for his next work.

The central incident at the beginning of *Heart and Science* matches the opening action of *Basil*, published thirty years earlier. The hero, moving through the streets of London, is overpowered by an unexpected emotion: love at first sight. Ovid Vere, unlike Basil, would have encountered the object of his love, Carmina Graywell, even without spotting her on the street. She is a cousin on her way to live under the guardianship of Ovid's mother, Mrs Gallilee, who tries to prevent Carmina and Ovid's marriage in order to inherit more of her ward's fortune. Carmina's religious belief scarcely enters the story, and her nurse Teresa's praying to the saints is more satirical than anything. Not much about this plot sounds like an anti-vivisection thesis, which is the label most often used to categorise *Heart and Science*. Ovid Vere, however, is a medical man, and in spinning out the romantic plot, Collins enters late nineteenth-century debates about experimentation upon live animals in the name of scientific or medicinal progress. Just as he consulted friends and experts regarding the factual details of his earlier novels, for this one he corresponded with Frances Power Cobbe, a leading voice against vivisection who proved to be an excellent source of information on the practice.

Ovid Vere's antagonist is Dr Benjulia who, while Ovid restores his own health in Canada, delays treating Carmina's nervous disorder because he believes he will learn more from watching the illness run its course. Benjulia's callousness emerges in his first appearance at the zoological gardens that the Gallilee household has come to tour. His errand is to collect a sick monkey, and he declines an offer of introduction to Carmina by unceremoniously declaring, 'I'd rather see the monkey.' Collins, as he explains in a preface, avoids taking readers into Benjulia's laboratory to witness the specific horrors of vivisection that await the monkey, and he refrains from excessive lecturing on the subject. The novel provides enough of a glimpse of the animals' suffering to motivate readers' sympathies and, most effectively, illustrates how the practice of torturing animals in the name of 'Knowledge' turns

Benjulia into a compassionless human. Significantly, the cure for Carmina's disorder comes from a 'mulatto' in the southern United States who, on his deathbed, has entrusted Ovid Vere with a groundbreaking medical manuscript. Vere's publication of the treatise proves to Benjulia that methods of inquiry avoiding vivisection are most successful. The key to restoring Carmina's health also echoes one of Collins' early works, *Mr Wray's Cash Box*. In both works, the traumatised and partially amnesiac patient must not be reminded of the actual event that triggered the breakdown.

Collins' stance on science in this novel complicates one's understanding of his views on the topic in general. He was always captivated by the workings of the mind, evidenced not only by his experimentation with mesmerism, but also in his novels' exploration of human psychology. *The Moonstone* advocates for science, with Ezra Jennings overcoming suspicion of the experiment and social dislike of his visible racial mixture simultaneously. In *Heart and Science*, Dr Benjulia is a similar spectacle at six foot six inches tall with a 'true gipsy-brown' complexion and the jet black hair of an 'American Indian', but his scientific views are vilified. With the solution in this novel coming from a 'mulatto', Collins avoids placing multiracial characters on either the righteous or the evil side of scientific advancement. Rather, he aligns and stacks ambiguities, which highlights the ways in which multiple signifiers of identity and morality complicate acts of reading. The novels consequently force readings not only at the superficial level of race or rank, but also at a deeper level of character and integrity.

Reviewers of *Heart and Science*, which appeared in several newspapers from July of 1882 to January of 1883 then slightly later in *Belgravia*, were unimpressed but not outraged. Their positions were as inconsistent as the novel itself, complaining that the book was too preoccupied with speaking out against vivisection yet also noting that many of the parts focused on vivisection were easily forgettable. With two explanatory prefaces, the book provided ample grounds for complaints about Collins' refusal to let the work speak for itself. Reviewers noted the skilful drawing of Dr Benjulia as well as Zo, a developmentally slow and amusingly forthright child. Miss Minerva, a governess with the type of conflicted motives that made Lydia Gwilt so intriguing, rounds out a list of the novel's most memorable characters.

The uneven reception that greeted *Heart and Science* was better than what lay in store for the next stage production Collins floated. The audience at the opening of *Rank and Riches* at the Adelphi on 9th June 1883 found the play so incomprehensible that they heckled the actors in mid-performance. Badly written lines and what *The Times* called 'outrageous improbability' were to blame (11th June 1883). Collins' cast was talented, but they could not rescue its bizarre characters, including a 'bird-doctor', from a melodrama whose multiple stories of bigamy appeared preposterous. This debacle did not result from a theatre company indulging the whims of an ailing but famous author and playwright; no one involved in the production, nor others who were familiar with the script, anticipated such failure. Collins continued to believe in the work and faulted the audience's lack of sophistication, but no more of his plays made it to the stage in his lifetime.

'*I Say No*' followed *Heart and Science*, returning Collins to crime and detection. The novel's mystery revolves around the orphaning of Emily Brown, a strong-minded and beautiful heroine. Various relatives and friends lead Emily to believe that her father dies suddenly of a heart condition to avoid exposing her to the shock of his apparently brutal murder. After unexpectedly sharing a room at an inn with a stranger, Mr Brown is discovered with his throat forcefully slashed, an act that reappears in *Blind Love* and suggests that Collins was continually disturbed by Ned Ward's bloody suicide. Next to Mr Brown lies the bloody razor of the now missing stranger, who appears to have absconded with Mr Brown's pocketbook. Various bits of evidence that fall into Emily Brown's path lead to her to the discovery that her father killed himself after reading a letter rejecting his marriage proposal. The letter simply states, 'I say no', providing the novel's cryptic title and pointing to the book's actual villain.

The novel's most harmful force is the internalised shame of sexual double standards and hypocrisy rather than a mean-spirited villainous individual. Mr Brown's love interest, Miss Sara Jethro, is a fallen woman who refuses to allow a restoration of her reputation. She insists upon punishing herself even though her beloved regards true repentance as sufficient castigation. In addition to another sympathetic rendering of a fallen woman, Collins revisits the topics of post-traumatic memory loss, love at first sight, infatuated drawing masters, and women detective figures. Motivated by the pure desire to ensure that her father's alleged murderer faces justice, Emily knows that the men she would have to approach in her investigation would either take liberties with or rebuff her, leaving her 'the most helpless hopeless creature on the wide surface of the earth – a girl self-devoted to the task of a man' (Ch LII). Collins also flirts with homoeroticism in the relationship between Emily and her schoolmate Cecilia, a dynamic peculiarly signalled in the stories that Francine, a mixed race character, repeats from Sappho – her 'mulatto' slave in the West Indies.

Notwithstanding these qualities, the novel on the whole is mediocre sensation fiction. Collins himself even mocks the sensational and melodramatic modes in which he writes as he describes a servant who pauses 'to see what effect she produced' while relaying the deathbed mumblings of Emily's aunt. The speaker then 'lifted one hand with theatrical solemnity – and luxuriously terrified herself with her own horrors' (Ch XV). Between December of 1883 and the end of 1884, 'I Say No' was serialised in multiple papers, including *Harper's Weekly* in the United States and *London Society*. As reviewers pointed out, Collins did not supplement the easily guessed mystery with enough complexity of character or plot to distinguish the work. Throughout the novel's composition, Collins was barely strong enough to keep up with the fast pace of publication deadlines. On 3rd May 1884, he turned down a request for work from George Bentley of *Temple Bar*, explaining: 'recent illness has thrown me back in my work. The weekly demand of the newspapers is inexorable – and my hours of rest (the doctor says) must be strictly observed. In this case, my own feeling of fatigue at the end of the day, sides with the doctor.' With maladies like toothaches added to his regular poor health, Collins seems to have fallen back on familiar themes without the fortitude to depict them in ever more nuanced ways.

Collins' letters from this period show a constant and unavoidable preoccupation with health, and he regularly found his limitations perturbing. A stark contrast to his earlier self, joining Dickens on long walks or jaunting around Paris with Ward, Collins was now bent over, using a stick to walk, and frail. Angina caused him uncomfortable chest pain, and he even had to scale back his diet. He tried all sorts of remedies in his constant battle with gout, sometimes settling into effective routines. Writing to his friend the actor and playwright George Rowe, Wilkie explained, 'A walk – a perspiration – five minutes in a warm bath – fierce rubbing on coming out – are the preventive remedies which succeed best, in my case' (21st February 1884). From August to September of 1884, he benefited from quite a bit of sailing, which he referred to as 'a good <u>salting</u> on board a friend's yacht' (13th October 1884). As soon as his joints improved, though, the inflammation often moved to his eyes. He was so frustrated sometimes that he could barely keep his pen from cursing. He wrote to his friend Jane Bigelow, 'One morning I was awakened by a little uneasiness in one of my eyes. I looked in the glass and saw the xxxxxxx gout (I am writing to a lady, and put crosses to represent the forcible expression of my feelings) – I say I saw the (blank) Gout in possession of my eye – in such obstinate possession, so often returning, that I am afraid to say positively that I am cured yet' (29th December 1884). The 'x' marks and Collins' insistence on insulting the gout, even with an articulated '(blank)', highlight how defiant the very act of writing had become for him.

Visits to Ramsgate in the summer and autumn of 1885 meant to 'oxygenise' his blood did Wilkie good. He kept two sets of lodgings, one for each family, and the children bounced between the houses. A letter that he dictated to Caroline mentions little Charley's presence with them as a matter of course (23rd October 1885). Despite his improvement, Wilkie sometimes disliked the mood of the place. Sounding like more of a cantankerous old man than he regarded himself, he wrote to his friend A.P. Watt, who had been his literary agent for three and a half years, 'My departure is hastened by the infernal noises which make this otherwise delightful place a hell upon earth. Organs – brass bands – howling costermongers selling fish, make day hideous – and night, too, up to 10 o'clock. Nobody complains but me' (24th June 1885).

In early 1884, Collins was reading the autobiography of Anthony Trollope, another very prolific novelist whom he visited and who had died just over a year earlier. Collins wrote to Watt, 'I could not read it through. The first part I thought very interesting – but when he sits in judgment on his own novels and on other peoples' novels he tells me what I don't want to know, and I bid him goodbye half way through the journey' (30th January 1884). The role of critic, which he himself donned in the early 1850s writing reviews for *The Leader*, was one that put Wilkie on edge at the end of his career. The inconsistent reception of his work in the 1880s probably made him more sensitive to smarting reviews. Rather than reflecting on his oeuvre, or the literary merits of other novelists' legacies, Collins focused more of his later years on mentoring younger aspiring writers, including the journalist Harry Quilter as well as the popular novelist Hall Caine, and on protecting fellow practitioners of the craft from copyright infringement.

Led by Walter Besant, Collins was a founding member of the Society of Authors in 1884. With Alfred Lord Tennyson as the

Society's first President, authors from both sides of the Atlantic united to try to strengthen copyright protections and enforcement. Collins and others had complained for years that they had no recourse when unauthorised copies of their works were sold for profit in the United States, and he had been victorious in late 1869 in pressuring the Belinfantine Brothers, Dutch publishers, to cut him a share of the profits for their publication of *Man and Wife*. Having negotiated publication contracts and translation agreements carefully for decades, and with a fair amount of legal knowledge, Collins understood the complexities of international literary negotiations and the early struggle to retain control over what we now call intellectual property.

Unable to move about in society as freely as he had in his stronger years, Collins did continue to make new friends in his final years. Mary Anderson, an American actress, grew close to Wilkie after their meeting in early 1885. Wilkie's spirits were so buoyed by the beautiful 25-year-old that he often visited Mary when he was too ill to want to see others, and she recalled him fondly in her memoirs, *A Few Memories* (1896). Another new young friend was a girl near the age of Collins' son. Anne le Poer Wynne, called 'Nannie', was about twelve years old when Collins befriended her widowed mother, Emily Wynne. Wilkie and Nannie exchanged a fascinating series of letters, beginning in May of 1885 and lasting until 1888, in which they constructed an elaborate story about being married and having children, with Wilkie addressing Nannie as 'Mrs Collins'. Collins also corresponded with Emily, who was privy to all of her daughter's correspondence and present during personal visits. Wilkie constantly commented in a jesting tone on Nannie's age as well as his own. There is no evidence of an actual romantic affair between Collins and the young girl, but the epistolary conceit of a marriage does strike one as odd. Fanciful and apparently harmless, the imagined marriage was a strange way for a man who wanted to encourage others to be dismissive of the institution to set up his relationship with an impressionable young girl. Had

Collins been conventionally married, the whole joke would be more apt to strike one as a grandfatherly fiction meant to divert a fatherless adolescent girl. Because Collins was so unconventional in his own affairs, it is tempting for readers to add the Wynne correspondence to the list of Collins' scandalous traits, but the epistolary evidence more convincingly suggests that the Wynne friendship was an outlet for Collins' sense of humour and a source of lighthearted emotional comfort for a dying man.

Playful on the subject of marriage with Nannie, Collins turned serious about it again in the novel he was writing. Recalling the deathbed pronouncements pointing witnesses to hidden letters that appear in so much sensation fiction, including Collins' *Black and White*, *The Evil Genius* begins with just such a scene. This account contains a double deathbed revelation: the dying and wrongly imprisoned Roderick Westerfield directs his wife to a letter containing the deathbed confession of yet another man as well as a paper written in undecipherable code specifying the location of some stolen diamonds. Mrs Westerfield, a greedy former barmaid, fails in her attempt to steal the diamonds and abandons the daughter she has abused for ten years when she departs for the United States with her son, who is later orphaned. The novel's heroine is the profoundly neglected daughter, Sydney Westerfield.

Contributing to the many 'governess novels' of the period that ponder the romantic consequences of hiring attractive young women to instruct the children of attractive older men, Collins' plot places the sexually innocent Syd in the household of the upstanding Mr Herbert Linley. Mrs Linley trusts Herbert and Syd implicitly, but her mother, Mrs Presty, immediately foresees that Syd will lure Herbert's affections away from his wife. Although Herbert sexually initiates the unsuspecting Syd and repeatedly chooses to satisfy his lust, he is never a candidate for the 'evil genius' label of the novel's title. In this context, 'genius' refers to the influencing spirits (good and evil) thought to guide an individual's behaviour, and Mrs Presty, rather than Syd or

Herbert, ultimately receives that designation. After their scandalous divorce has been executed, the novel's conclusion reunites Mr and Mrs Linley in marriage. Neither Mrs Westerfield nor the saga of the diamonds figure significantly in the rest of the story, and although Collins demarcates that plot by titling it 'Before the Story', one sign of his narrative powers waning is the absence of resolution for many of the points raised in the novel's intriguing opening. Inexplicably, the compassionate Syd never undertakes to find the little brother from whom she is cruelly separated. Collins' writing is also uneven; he shows an uncharacteristic lack of inventiveness, repeating the word 'delicious', for instance, to describe everything from air to confusion to a child's sleep. Yet other passages display Collins' powers of description as impressively as ever. Of the gardens at a Sydenham hotel, he writes, 'Even the amateur artist could take liberties with Nature, and find the accommodating limits of the garden sufficient for his purpose. Trees in the foreground sat to him for likenesses that were never recognised; and hills submitted to unprovoked familiarities, on behalf of brushes which were not daunted by distance' (Ch XLIII).

Full of purely sensational components, including the notion that seeing the face of a departed governess will rescue a child from typhus, *The Evil Genius* is entertaining if not subtle. Its ultimate stance on divorce simultaneously invites and discourages readers to speculate about Collins' own position on the subject. Two respected characters conclude by asserting that women should not be granted legal divorces due to a husband's 'sexual frailty' or infidelity. Instead, wives should be upstanding Christians and forgive truly repentant spouses. In the light of suffragist movements and the continued updating of the Matrimonial Causes Act of 1857, which established secular divorce, this position harks back to a very traditionalist attitude. Immediately after presenting this opinion and recapping the divorce then remarriage of Mr and Mrs Linley, the family lawyer asks, 'Where is the novelist who would be bold enough to invent such an incident as this? Never mind the novelist' ('After the Story'). Perhaps Collins is suggesting that his own views on marriage, an institution whose value he ceaselessly criticised, do not necessarily match those of his characters. Reviewers noted that this good book paled in comparison to Collins' great ones, but his reputation was hardly a shambles. Even after citing the novel's weak points, *The Academy*'s anonymous reviewer called Collins 'the greatest living master of narrative, pure and simple' (2nd October 1886). Indeed, the breaks between instalments of the serialised text occur at the most suspenseful of moments. The novel appeared in multiple newspapers owned by Tillotson & Sons beginning in December of 1885, and Collins was frustrated that it took until September of 1886 for it to appear in book form. On 30th October 1885, just one performance of *The Evil Genius* took place at the Vaudeville Theatre to secure Collins' copyright. He wrongly expected that other theatre companies would pick up the show, and composing the work as a play and a novel at the same time had taxed his strength.

The emotional toll of Collins' fluctuating health strikingly appears in two letters from December 1885. On the 13th, Collins wrote to Watt, 'For the first time, for years past, I can write with a pencil which doesn't try my temper, and I can smell the true cedar perfume when I open the box which doubles my present and my pleasure. Between what I owe to you, and to the delicious cold weather (oh, may it last!) I am beginning to feel so young again that I don't believe I was born in the year 1824.' Just six days later, he wrote to Emily Wynne, 'The cruel change in the weather has knocked <u>me</u> down most effectually. I get up to write the "weekly part" of *The Evil Genius* which must be written – and then tumble down again, a heap of helpless mortality that sleeps badly, eats badly, and behaves badly as a correspondent.' The poignant contrast between hope and despondency is heartrending. Writing agonised Wilkie, but it also usefully prevented him from staying in bed all day. Late in 1886, he forced himself into twelve-hour work days to complete a Christmas number for Arrowsmith's. The gruelling pace that fatigued him yet helped him find purpose did not produce a great novella.

In *The Guilty River*, Gerard Roylake returns from his education on the Continent to inherit Trimley Deen, where he falls in love with Cristel Toller, the daughter of a miller whose cottage abuts the estate. A nameless man called 'the Deaf Lodger' has also fallen in love with Toller at first sight, and he irrationally threatens all rivals with death regardless of Cristel's utter lack of feeling for him. The Lodger, who asks to be called 'the Cur' because he is a 'mixed breed', faces a mid-life crisis as he ponders which of his lineages will determine his fate. In a mash-up of Collins' favourite themes, the Lodger's crisis forces him to confront deafness as well as his family's sordid past. After his mother's sudden death, an illness causes the man to lose his hearing slowly. When he is almost completely deaf, he finally understands what is happening in the least appropriate and unintentionally humorous of ways: a nurse shouts the information into his ear. His beloved mother, a slave freed in her master's deathbed will, leaves a packet of papers explaining that the moral taint on the Lodger's name comes not from his slave heritage but from his white male ancestors. That lineage reveals a paternal grandfather hanged for wilful murder, an uncle killed in a duel for gambling with 'loaded dice', and a father whose abandonment of a pregnant mistress he had promised to marry leads her to drown herself and her child.

The novella's portrait of hearing loss is sympathetic and as accurately treated as blindness in *Poor Miss Finch*. The character flaws that develop with the frustrating physical disability, however, also lead the Lodger to follow the path of the corrupted white men when he attempts to murder Gerard out of jealousy. The restoration of the Lodger's hearing restores the 'spirit' of his mother's 'sweet nature', and his regained sense of morality leads him to share Cristel's address with Gerard, which enables the resolution of the romance plot (Ch XVIII). The novella also features a suspenseful escape scene, biting satire of aristocratic

English society, and sensational moments of poisoning, rescue, and romance, but Collins' haste in writing resulted in clumsy transitioning between such elements. Sales were bad, and Wilkie later agreed with a friend that the story was 'spoilt for want of room' (30th July 1887).

Collins felt close to death and endured domestic upheaval while composing his last complete novel, *The Legacy of Cain*. On 20th December 1887, he reported to Watt, 'On Sunday last I very nearly put a premature end to "the Legacy of Cain". In other words, I went out for a walk – and in two minutes the detestable raw air caught my heart, or my lungs, or both – I staggered back as nearly <u>suffocated</u> as a man could well be.' After this incident, he was unable to leave the house for several weeks, but by early January, he could take short walks. Wilkie had assumed he would live at Gloucester Place indefinitely, but when his landlord charged too much for renewal of the twenty-one-year-old lease, Wilkie tolerated an unwelcome disturbance of his routine in order to move house in March. With copious complaint, he took smaller quarters for himself and Caroline at 82 Wimpole Street, which was further from Martha Rudd and the children. Also in March and still in the midst of writing, the proud grandfather to Carrie's four daughters was greatly saddened by the death of Carrie's youngest infant. The families were close, with Wilkie's grandchildren playing often with his children by Martha, and he worried about the depth of Carrie's loss.

As he continued writing *The Legacy of Cain*, Collins routinely told friends that he was not sure he would live to complete the book and that its attempt might hasten his end. To Watt, he wrote, 'You shall hear when I have finished the work – unless the work finishes <u>me</u>' (9th May 1888). Wilkie kept the upper hand, and the story was syndicated in Tillotson's newspapers, beginning with *The Leigh Journal and Times*, from February to June of 1888. Carrie's position of honour as the novel's dedicatee is not surprising, given that she was a faithful daughter and served as a reliable amanuensis for several years, but it is doubly interesting because the novel's storyline concerns adoptees. The plot revolves around an experiment in which a minister, Abel Gracedieu, raises his biological daughter Helena with an adopted girl, Eunice, whose mother was a murderer. Implausibly, neither girl knows which one was adopted. Gracedieu hopes to prove wrong a doctor who insists that Eunice is destined to follow her mother's path, and Eunice succeeds in resisting the negative impulses she is sometimes provoked to feel without knowing that such impulses stem from her mother. Helena is the one who ultimately attempts murder, but the story's depiction of her deranged mother's influence undercuts Abel Gracedieu's rhetorical victory. As its title suggests, the novel is concerned with the potential hereditary nature of criminality, a subject that had puzzled Collins since his earliest writings. Yet his talents had diminished so considerably that reviewers who continued to praise him as one of the greatest storytellers in England were forced to admit that the novel lacked spark and humour. Collins was unsure of the book's reception but, unwilling to blame himself entirely, faulted the tastes of simple readers in the way he had reproached the unreceptive audience of *Rank and Riches*.

Death again threatened Collins while he was working on *Blind Love*, a novel he would not finish himself. Shortly after his sixty-fifth birthday, Collins was in a terrible cab accident. He described being surrounded by flying glass and thrown from the cab, but, amazingly, he was not cut or seriously injured when he collected himself on the grass (23rd January 1889). Remaining in generally poor health, plagued by bronchitis and his usual pains, Collins was able to continue working on *Blind Love*, but sometime in the spring he thought it prudent to construct a detailed outline of the book from Chapter XLI onward. The novel was originally called *Iris*, which he abandoned then folded into what was eventually called *Blind Love*.

Based on the case of Baron Von Scheurer, who perpetrated a complicated international insurance fraud, the novel also attacks Irish Nationalism. Set partially in Ireland in 1881, the plot speaks directly to the Land War that took place from 1879 to '82. Lord Harry, a stereotypical portrait of the 'wild Irishman' in contrast to calm and rational English counterparts, is the novel's villain. Until very late in drafting, this character's name had supplanted its heroine's for a title, but Collins changed it to avoid potential opposition to the vulgar slang term for the devil. Iris, illustrative of the final title concept, follows her passion when she marries Harry after his debts lead him to a bloody suicide attempt. Her devotion later prevents her from seeing that Harry has participated in murderous fraud until her maid, Fanny Mere, exposes the full extent of his treachery. Fanny Mere brings us one last flash of Collins' appreciation for the delights of women's bodies. Admiring some of Napoleon Sarony's drawings, Collins wrote, '… I too think the back view of a finely-formed woman the loveliest view – and her hips the most precious parts of that view' (29th March 1887). True to her author's fantasy, Fanny Mere has a backside pleasing enough to attract men who see her first from the rear.

Collins had intended to publish this novel quickly in the summer of 1887, prior to *The Legacy of Cain*, but poor health and other commitments delayed its appearance in *The Illustrated London News* to 6th July 1889, when he was in serious decline. On 30th June, Wilkie survived a severe stroke. Suffering from paralysis on his left side, he was also nervous and mentally distressed for weeks. On 4th August, Carrie worried that her father would expire at any moment, and she reported to Watt that Wilkie 'took no nourishment or <u>anything</u> for 26 hours'.[10] Collins rallied, and his wit returned, but he knew that he could not finish the novel. In a reversal of the incident in 1862 when Collins declined Dickens' offer to complete *No Name*, at Collins' request Walter Besant finished *Blind Love* using the meticulously detailed plan in the notebook. Collins had written forty-eight of the sixty-four chapters, leaving Besant to complete seven and a half of the twenty-six weekly parts, which he did swiftly, including every bit of dialogue that Collins had carefully placed in the notebook outline.

In September, Wilkie could write a bit in his own diary, and he wrote or dictated some letters to friends, including notes that bid farewell. As the weeks progressed and his condition worsened, his letters tried to keep an upbeat attitude, but it seems that he recognised the late stages of dying. Wilkie did not deny himself pleasure at the end, taking time to enjoy a fine cigar even though his weak lungs required him to be propped up in an armchair. Caroline, Carrie, and a hired nurse did their best to keep him comfortable, and Dr Frank Beard lived close by for quick summoning at the very end. Wilkie Collins had once written of the 'foretaste of death which embitters all human partings', and on 23rd September 1889, his death finalised such a parting.[11] Caroline recorded the time, 10 a.m., in Wilkie's diary.

The funeral on 27th September drew many admirers. Caroline and Carrie were joined by Wilkie's close friends, including Francis Beard, Edward Pigott, Jane Ward, Ada Cavendish, and William Holman Hunt. Professional colleagues and friends included A.P. Watt, Edmund Yates, Hall Caine, and Charles Dickens' eldest son. Mamie Dickens, the eldest daughter, thoughtfully sent a wreath of red geraniums, Dickens' favourite flower, and Kate (now Perugini, having remarried since Charley Collins' death) sent flowers as well. Martha Rudd sent a wreath under the Dawson family alias. Several of Collins' fans appeared at the cemetery, reportedly carrying Wilkie's books in their arms.

Illustrating how life stories continue to unfold even over a century following one's death, the most recent discussions of Collins' funeral suggest a dramatic new possibility. Graham Law and Andrew Maunder recently publicised a death notice from an American newspaper, *The World*, which had previously received little if any attention. 'Wilkie Collins' Last Days', published anonymously on 29th September 1889, not only explains that Collins' will provided for Martha and her children, which points to a source very close to the estate because the will had not yet been made public, but also states that Martha and the children were present at the funeral. If such an account is true, it has the potential to radically change our understanding of the family's relationships because Martha's presence at the funeral may suggest that Collins' lovers were already on familiar footing. The funeral would surely seem a difficult place for a first face-to-face meeting. Since Martha's children were frequently present in Caroline's household, it seems more likely that if both women were at the funeral, it was not the first time they had spotted one another.

Wilkie Collins was buried at Kensal Green Cemetery, where he and Caroline planned for her to join him upon her death. No monument marks Caroline's burial there, which took place in 1895. Their union remains as publicly unacknowledged in death as it was in life. The grave marker of white stone says only 'In Memory of Wilkie Collins, Author of The Woman in White and Other Works of Fiction', followed by the dates of his birth and death under a large cross. Collins himself left instructions for the inscription in his will, choosing to secure the legacy of his beloved novel beside his identity as a storyteller. His relationship to his writing was one in which he sometimes toiled at the mercy of a plot and sometimes presided over it with more control. He once wrote to Anne Procter, 'I have been tied to The Woman in White's petticoat string, like a dog to his kennel. The reward of this solitary confinement under a female turnkey is not far off' (23rd July 1860). Likening the novel to a prison, Collins clearly felt that, even though the story was his own creation, it took over and controlled his external surroundings. Rather differently, The Guilty River was a tale at his mercy when he described having to close a letter due to internal creative agitation: 'My new story is knocking at my head, and saying, "Why don't you let me out?"' (26th July 1886). From the moment he appeared in the cradle, Wilkie Collins' head seems to have been bulging with stories, and over the course of his life, sometimes straining himself well past the point of exhaustion, he committed himself to making sure that he liberated as many of the tales as he could. In over twenty novels, several plays, and countless short stories, Collins thrilled, perplexed, surprised, and thoroughly entertained his audience. These stories may no longer rattle Wilkie Collins' head, but they certainly continue to knock about in ours.

Legacies

The most immediately significant piece of Collins' writing that came to light posthumously was his last will and testament. Having invented names for himself and his lovers for decades to avoid publicised exposure, Wilkie boldly outed both Caroline and Martha in his will. Collins, who had written so much about how marriage and property laws harmed women, was extremely specific in the document, making sure that Caroline, Martha, and all of the children were provided for equitably. He unambiguously acknowledged paternity of Marian, Harriet and Charley, revealing the Dawson alias and listing the houses in which they were born 'for the better identification of the said three children'. He had also made sure that all of his children received a good education, hoping that it would enable his daughters to retain more autonomy if they ever married, or to avoid marriage altogether. In Carrie's case, the institution her father so detested ultimately devastated her.

Collins did not have as much to bequeath as one would expect for someone of his stature. That he was a big spender and maintained comfortable lifestyles for both Martha Rudd and Caroline Graves was only part of the reason. Carrie's husband, Henry Bartley, was another reason. After the marriage, Wilkie allowed the unscrupulous Bartley to handle his estate, which Bartley managed poorly and later plundered. A letter that Carrie wrote to A.P. Watt in 1901 would have stung Wilkie to the heart. In it, she begged Watt to help her sell Wilkie's travelling desk, which he had made as a replica of Dickens', for any sum because she and her daughters were going hungry trying to survive on the small bit of inheritance Mr Bartley had not taken.

Even after Marian and Harriet Dawson were named in their father's will, they never publicly revealed their parentage. The sisters died in the same year, 1955, when the revelation of their heritage would have been less socially catastrophic than during the Victorian period. Still, although neither woman had married nor mothered children, concern about a social taint being passed on to their niece and nephew may have prevented them from claiming the Collins connection. Wilkie and Martha's son Charley married and had two children, from whom the only known living relatives of Wilkie Collins are directly descended.

Although Collins had requested a simple funeral, some of his friends were convinced (and conceivably encouraged by Collins' gravestone inscription) that he would not object to additional monuments honouring his literary achievements. Harry Quilter publicly solicited donations for a memorial he hoped to erect in Westminster Abbey, turning to St Paul's Cathedral when that plan failed. Donations were slow to accumulate, and St Paul's Dean and Chapter balked at the idea, holding a low opinion of Collins' artistic stature and disapproving of his lifestyle. The funds Quilter had gathered eventually established the Wilkie Collins Memorial Library of Fiction at the People's Palace, which later became Queen Mary's College, but the books in the library have not survived.

As was the case for many Victorian novelists, appreciation of Collins' novels waned during the late nineteenth and early twentieth centuries when the popularity of Victorian fiction was considered a mark of its status as a 'low' form of art. Collins' literary legacy also suffered as the result of the critical tendency to regard him, often inaccurately, as an inferior protégé of Dickens. Besides the error of drawing a comparison by isolating two individual figures out of the sea of reputable nineteenth-century novelists

(Braddon, the Brontës, Eliot, Reade, Thackeray, Trollope, Wood) whose works were often in close conversation, approaches aimed at defining the 'better' novelist often mistakenly assume that the writers were attempting to outdo one another. Although competitive natures made themselves known, Victorian novelists also frequently went out of their way to praise and even promote each other's works. The writers of Collins' obituaries for the most part avoided some of the missteps of later critics by paying appropriate tribute to his central works, noting that not all of his later fiction was poor, and making plain that Collins was as much of an influence on the famous Dickens as Dickens was on Collins. T.S. Eliot's 'Wilkie Collins and Dickens' (1927) began to rekindle respect for Collins as a novelist, as Eliot commented positively on melodrama, elevating the genre and Collins himself as an individual practitioner. Following Eliot's essay, scholarly attention to Collins gradually increased over the course of the twentieth century with biographies and critical studies slowly building upon each other. One benchmark of the resurgent interest was the founding of the Wilkie Collins Society in 1980, and the intensified attention Collins' work began to receive in the final two to three decades of the twentieth century continues today.

The Moonstone and *The Woman in White* have made their way into many literary canons, and now entire university courses are taught on sensation fiction. Several of Collins' novels, even some of the ones considered obscure, are in print and easily available from reputable presses, including Broadview, Oxford, and Penguin. Book-length studies and collections of essays address a wide range of topics, including Collins and human psychology, Collins and women, and Collins' importance in the traditions of Gothic and sensation fiction. No respectable comprehensive study of detective or crime fiction can omit Wilkie Collins, and discussion of his works has increasingly appeared alongside consideration of works by Dickens, Eliot, Thackeray, and Trollope in retrospectives and theories of the Victorian novel. A *Cambridge Companion to Wilkie Collins* was published in 2006, and persistent curiosity about his life has merited the continued publication of his letters, which is sure to fuel even more innovative studies. Collins' artistic presence as a novelist, journalist and playwright as well as the wide-ranging social concerns present in his writing make his life and work a continually rich resource for those investigating just about any aspect of the Victorian era.

Because Collins influenced the development of multiple literary genres, most especially detective, crime, and sensation fiction, countless titles – explicitly or silently – follow in his wake. Sir Arthur Conan Doyle's stories are indebted to Collins, and many have noted *The Moonstone*'s Sergeant Cuff as Sherlock Holmes' predecessor. The widely read works of Agatha Christie belong to the same tradition. Given these developments, it is often difficult to remember that there was a time when to write a novel focused on a detective solving a crime was new. There was a first time that a popular detective story ('The Biter Bit') was written entirely in the form of letters. Certain types of devices and plots, the 'locked room crime' for instance, have now become so clichéd that it is often difficult to remember that they have not always existed and that Collins' works were among the first to strike out in such directions. His 'firsts' remain, to this day, some of the best examples of the form.

In addition to crime and mystery authors, writers of historical fiction set in the nineteenth century have increasingly noticed Wilkie Collins. The influence is most direct in the works of writers such as Anne Perry who pen historical crime fiction set in Victorian London, but, just as Collins' books extended well beyond the arena of crime, so do those of his successors. The influence of novelists like Collins, Dickens, and Eliot, for instance, is apparent in some of the best historical fiction of the early twenty-first century, such as Michel Faber's *The Crimson Petal and the White* and Sarah Waters' *Fingersmith*, both published in 2002.

In *Fingersmith*, Waters riffs on Collins' plot from *The Woman in White* as more than one protagonist faces the threat of incarceration in a madhouse. One woman's imprisonment under a false identity powerfully illustrates the real madness of trying to prove one's true identity when the claiming of that identity has been diagnosed as the primary symptom of one's lunacy. Waters' carefully researched account of the inside of the asylum illuminates tortures that most Victorian readers would have refused to confront, and the novel's use of the inmate's point of view avoids a preachy or pedantic tone. The horror is too raw to need pontification. With infant impostors placed in upper-class homes, shocking revelations about presumably moral gentry folk, and profound questioning of whether biological or social bonds are strongest, Waters manages to update the sensation genre, keeping its shocking elements but with less strained plausibility. Revelations that initially appear surprising turn out to have been plotted by a criminal mastermind. In this excellently written novel, Waters shares Collins' skill in managing multiple narrators as well as his desire to sympathise with disempowered women and to challenge readers' expectations regarding 'normal' sexual behaviour.

James Wilson's *The Dark Clue* (2001) lifts actual characters from *The Woman in White*, following Walter Hartright and Marian Halcombe past the concluding events of Collins' book. The novel immediately hooks readers with an epigram in which the author explains that the manuscript may only be discovered once he and his closest relations are dead. Wilson then manages to invoke Collins and Dickens on the first page with the description of a street scene drowning in the type of thick fog that opens Dickens' *Bleak House*. *The Dark Clue*'s plot has Walter, with Marian's help, researching a biography of the acclaimed yet mysterious Romantic painter J.M.W. Turner. Motivated in part by hints in the paintings, Walter descends into disreputable spheres of Victorian society as he investigates what Turner may have hidden from the public. The minutiae of Turner's paintings may captivate students and admirers of Romantic art, but even though such details are part of the plot's development, the novel loses much of its momentum if a reader is not already familiar with the artistic works as well as *The Woman in White*. Wilson also uses Collins' device of alternating narrative voices and modes with letters and diaries, but he fails to provide enough stylistic variance to distinguish the voices well.

Another vein of historical fiction has used Wilkie Collins as a character in recreations of Victorian London. The stories we continue to hear about Collins – the details of his life that continue to motivate discoveries as well as the details we imagine or invent – tell us as much about ourselves as they do about Collins. For each retelling reveals much about the types of life narratives we are most invested in finding. This point is especially salient in fictionalisations of Collins himself. Repeatedly, these writers emphasise Collins' sexual appetite and the procurement of prostitutes over, for instance, the kindheartedness and cheerful demeanour that his friends noted as so personally distinctive. Writers of historical fiction also frequently place Collins in the most lurid of opium dens rather than the more mundane places where Collins actually procured and used his laudanum: in his own home and from the establishments of sanctioned providers or medical men.

Death by Dickens (2004), a short story collection edited by Anne Perry, includes two pieces with characters from the Collins family. Martin Edwards' 'The House of the Red Candle' uses what has become a familiar narrative conceit, presenting the story as an excerpt from Collins' own private papers. Concern for a prostitute leads Collins and Dickens to a brothel where a suspected murderess seems to have disappeared impossibly, and their slowly developing detective skills result in an entertaining exposition of the mystery. Peter Tremayne's 'The Passing Shadow' partners not Wilkie but Charley Collins uncomfortably with his father-in-law investigating another murder, this one with details the story posits as the inspiration for parts of both Dickens' *Our Mutual Friend* and Collins' *The Moonstone*. Edwards' and Tremayne's stories in this collection, perhaps because their short length precludes expectations that the characters be developed deeply, are entertaining if not complex. Writers of longer fiction have also mined the rich imaginative potential of Collins' friendship with Dickens. The many unanswered questions that persist about the particularities of the friendship make it a ripe place to imagine or to begin a novel. Contemporary writers, again seeming to reveal more about their views of authorship than about Collins himself, tend to assume and emphasise jealousy and bitterness towards Dickens on Collins' part.

Multiple such works use the narrative device of the lost or hidden manuscript to frame the fiction, including William J. Palmer's series of novels featuring Collins, Dickens, and characters named after scholars of the Victorian period. The first in the series, *The Detective and Mr Dickens: Being An Account of the Macbeth Murders and the Strange Events Surrounding Them. A Secret Journal, Attributed to Wilkie Collins, Discovered and Edited by William J Palmer* (1991), has Collins joining Dickens and Inspector Charles Frederick Field of the Metropolitan Police Force in a murder investigation. For Victorianists, the book is something like a treasure hunt without a map as multiple characters turn up with names close to or matching those of colleagues; even the name of the philosopher Jacques Derrida turns up in the sexualised slang of a lewd song. A focused plot and some exciting chase sequences hold readers' attention, but historical inaccuracies, such as having Collins in contact with Dickens before the year in which the men met, problematise the reading experience for those well-versed in the period or wishing to learn about it. Also problematic are multiple sexually explicit or rape scenes that appear gratuitously detailed. Just as the men Palmer imagines refuse to grant subjectivity to the women they employ or violate, Palmer does not grant his exploited women characters sufficient inner lives or voices to match other supporting figures, such as Inspector Field. The series continues with titles targeting 'The Medusa Murders', a 'Feminist Phantom' and a seasonal 'Oxford Christmas Plot'.

More recently, Dan Simmons has taken up not only the Collins/Dickens friendship but also the themes of Dickens' unfinished final novel *The Mystery of Edwin Drood*, a work in which many see strong evidence of Collins' influence. In *Drood* (2009), Simmons uses Collins as his narrator and speculates that the central character of Dickens' last book emerged – whether literally or imaginatively is never fully clear – from the remains of a train wreck that Dickens survived in 1865. The book interestingly explores a manipulative and chess-like mental game between Collins, Dickens, and Inspector Field and includes some chilling scenes of ritualistic cults in the sewers beneath London. *Drood*'s extensive quoting of Collins' and Dickens' letters, however, as well as vast amounts of biographical information that does little or nothing to further the plot leaves the nearly eight-hundred-page novel without a definitive climax. Fans of Collins and readers familiar with the Victorian era may find it entertaining to speculate about his mindset during the years of heaviest opium use, but a murderous and misogynist Wilkie hardly feels consistent with the one that emerges from the surviving ephemera of his life.

Whether long or short, the historical fiction that attempts to depict Collins himself faces the challenge of trying to educate readers while also seeming natural to the nineteenth century. Often, these attempts result in speech patterns and declarations of facts that would have sounded ludicrous to an actual Victorian. For instance, the fictional Collins and Dickens tend to use one another's first names frequently enough to suggest that they have forgotten one another's identities. Phrases such as 'my dear Wilkie' and 'the Inimitable' may flow from the tongues of these fictional characters more times than they were ever spoken by Collins or Dickens in their lifetimes. At their weakest moments, some authors of historical fiction feel the need to have Wilkie make clumsy statements, such as, 'you are Dickens the Inimitable, the most famous writer in England', as if Dickens himself would not have been aware of his own status. Still, such works vividly remind contemporary readers how dramatically some characteristics of the Victorian world differed from our own and help to inspire the reading, or rereading, of the unforgettable novels that first made Wilkie Collins' name famous.

Those novels have also been envisioned in various ways by television and film producers. The early twentieth century saw many of Collins' novels on the silent screen, including *Armadale*, *The Dead Secret*, *The Moonstone*, and several versions of *The New Magdalen* and *The Woman in White*. Every decade or so, the BBC has produced a television version of either *The Woman in White* or *The Moonstone*, with the most recent versions appearing in the years 1997 and 1996 respectively. In 1998, Radha Bharadwaj wrote, directed and produced a film of *Basil* starring Jared Leto, Christian Slater and Sir Derek Jacobi. Just as Collins' novels remain in print in several languages, non-English-language television and film adaptations have emerged. The Swedish *Kvinna I Vitt* (1949), Russian *Zhenshchina V Belom* (1982) and Italian *La Donna in Bianco* (1980) are all versions of *The Woman in White*, and German television produced a mini-series of that novel as well as *Armadale* and *The Moonstone* in the 1970s. Viewers of such programmes do well to recall that, although Collins never appreciated unauthorised adaptations of his work, both because they could damage the reputation of his novels and because he received no remuneration, his objections were not based on the degree of change from the originals. Interpretive choices that stray far from the source texts may have been perfectly palatable to Collins, who radically changed his own plots when he staged them. Having himself removed the Indian characters from *The Moonstone*, for instance, Collins may not have been shocked at other changes, such as the erasure of Ezra Jennings' racial mixture, wrought by future directors.

Adaptations of Collins' work also continue to find their way to the stage, where directors necessarily take their own views of the plots and often change major scenes. The autumn of 2004 was a particularly active period. In September, an Andrew Lloyd

Webber musical production of *The Woman in White* opened at the Palace Theatre in London's West End. Directed by Trevor Nunn with lyrics by David Zippel, the very long musical was most noteworthy for its use of innovative and shifting projections in lieu of traditional sets. The changes to Marian Halcombe's character and the romance plot were far less satisfying than the thrilling vision of a locomotive barrelling towards audiences. Although reviews were mixed, the production ran to five hundred performances and earned five Olivier Award nominations in 2005, two of which it won. In November of 2005, a Broadway production opened at the Marquis Theatre. Despite closing after just three months, the show earned five Outer Critics Circle nominations as well as a 2006 Tony Award nomination for Webber's and Zippel's score.

Also in 2004, playwright Richard Cameron debuted *Gong Donkeys* at the Bush Theatre in London. A reworking of *The Lazy Tour of Two Idle Apprentices*, the play joins the story of Collins' and Dickens' trip to Doncaster with the tale of David, a contemporary teenager who must stay with relatives in that region while his mother recovers from a mental breakdown occasioned by a broken marriage. 'Gong donkey' was Dickens' term for drunken folks in the Doncaster crowds whose vocal effusions resembled the banging of a gong as well as a donkey's bray – a fitting and ironic title for a play about the potential power of storytelling. The character with an amateur interest in history relates Collins' ghost story from *The Lazy Tour*, and his obsession with the Dickens/Ternan affair in addition to the separation of David's parents invites one to reflect upon the relevance of such historically removed events to present lives.

A part of Collins' legacy worthy of increased attention in critical appraisals is the Society of Authors. The organisation, which Collins co-founded in 1884, remains an active advocate for the rights of authors in multiple media. In addition to providing information about intellectual property protection and copyright law, the Society helps to establish minimum payment terms with a number of publishers and assists in negotiating fees with the

BBC when all or part of an author's work is broadcast. In this way, the contributions of Collins and his colleagues have helped to advance an important social cause that continues to benefit literary professionals.

Learning about Wilkie Collins' life and career causes one to re-evaluate the extent to which some of the most famous people and most popular writings of the Victorian period defy oversimplified expectations. Collins' works are memorable for their shocks: a blue man, a villain with no legs, a pregnant woman rushing into Spanish war scenes, lovers who poison, and prostitutes who marry priests. The works endure because this strangeness is rarely gratuitous. Amidst the shock, Collins' writing demands deep questioning of disability, sexual double standards, myths of racial purity, and multiple forms of socially sanctioned oppression. The rebel, the outcast, or the struggling nonconformist, physically disabled or otherwise, was not only an unjustly persecuted figure but also an inescapable part of the social fabric. The inclusion of repellent as well as sympathetic misfits throughout Collins' body of work insists upon a diversity of difference and grants a flawed – and therefore accessible, recognisable – humanity to characters so often drawn in other fiction as one-dimensionally odd. These complexities, in addition to fast-paced and intriguing plots, continue to draw new readers to (and to inspire new imaginings of) Collins' tales. Exploring the power of lust, the inequities of marriage, a mysterious disappearance, or a comic scenario, the works of Wilkie Collins stand as a testament to the lasting and varied legacies of a supreme storyteller.

Notes

1. Charles Dickens to Georgina Hogarth, 25th November 1853.
2. Anonymous reviews in *The Athenaeum* 4th December 1852 and *The Westminster Review* October 1853, respectively.
3. To Georgina Hogarth 25th October 1853.
4. To Georgina Hogarth 25th November 1853.
5. To Georgina Hogarth 25th November 1853.
6. 12th July 1854.
7. Quoted in Peters, *The King of Inventors*, 435–7.
8. 29th October 1868.
9. Locker's letter of 25th January 1875 is printed in *The Public Face of Wilkie Collins,* Vol III, 65–66.
10. 5th August 1889. Carrie's letter is included in *The Public Face of Wilkie Collins,* Vol IV, 388.
11. *Heart and Science*, Ch XIX.

Selected works

Novels, Novellas and Non-Fiction

1848   *Memoirs of the Life of William Collins, Esq., R.A.*

1850   *Antonina; or, The Fall of Rome*

1851   *Rambles Beyond Railways; or, Notes in Cornwall Taken A-Foot*

1851   *Mr Wray's Cash Box; or, The Mask and the Mystery*

1852   *Basil: A Story of Modern Life*

1854   *Hide and Seek; or, The Mystery of Mary Grice*

1856   *A Rogue's Life* (1st–29th March in *Household Words*; revised for one-volume publication in 1879)

1857   *The Dead Secret* (3rd January–13th June in *Household Words*)

1857   *The Perils of Certain English Prisoners* (with Charles Dickens, Christmas number of *Household Words*)

1859   *The Woman in White* (26th November 1859–25th August 1860 in *All the Year Round*)

1862   *No Name* (15th March 1862–17th January 1863 in *All the Year Round*)

1864   *Armadale* (November 1864–June 1866 in *The Cornhill Magazine*)

1867   *No Thoroughfare* (with Charles Dickens, Christmas number of *All the Year Round*)

1868   *The Moonstone: A Romance* (4th January–8th August in *All the Year Round*)

1869   *Man and Wife* (November 1869–July 1870 in *Cassell's Magazine*)

1871   *Poor Miss Finch: A Novel* (2nd September 1871–24th February 1872 in *Cassell's Magazine*)

1871   *Miss or Mrs?* (Christmas number of *The Graphic*)

1872   *The New Magdalen* (October 1872–July 1873 in *Temple Bar*)

1874   *The Law and the Lady* (26th September 1874–13th March 1875 in *The Graphic*)

1876   *The Two Destinies: A Romance* (January–September in *Temple Bar*)

1877   *My Lady's Money: An Episode in the Life of a Young Girl* (Christmas number of *The Illustrated London News*)

1878   *The Haunted Hotel: A Mystery of Modern Venice* (June–November 1878 in *Belgravia Magazine*)

1879   *The Fallen Leaves* (1st January–23rd July in *The World*)

1879   *Jezebel's Daughter* (13th September 1879–31st January 1880 in *The Bolton Weekly Journal*)

1880   *The Black Robe* (2nd October 1880–26th March 1881 in *The Sheffield and Rotherham Independent*)

1882   *Heart and Science: A Story of the Present Time* (August 1882–June 1883 in *Belgravia Magazine*)

1884	*'I Say No': Or The Love-Letter Answered* (January–December in *London Society*)
1885	*The Evil Genius: A Domestic Story* (11th December 1885–30th April 1886 in *The Leigh Journal and Times*)
1886	*The Guilty River* (*Arrowsmith*'s Christmas Annual)
1888	*The Legacy of Cain* (17th February–29th June in *The Leigh Journal and Times*)
1889	*Blind Love* (6th July–28th December in *The Illustrated London News*; completed by Walter Besant)

Story Collections

1856	*After Dark*
1859	*The Queen of Hearts*
1863	*My Miscellanies*
1887	*Little Novels*

Drama

1855	*The Lighthouse*
1857	*The Frozen Deep*
1858	*The Red Vial*
1868	*No Thoroughfare*
1869	*Black and White*
1873	*Man and Wife*
1873	*The New Magdalen*
1883	*Rank and Riches*

Posthumous

| 1991 | *Ioláni, or Tahiti As It Was: A Romance* (written in 1844) |

Bibliography

Bachman, Maria K. and Don Richard Cox, ed., *Reality's Dark Light: The Sensational Wilkie Collins* (Knoxville, 2003)

Baker, William, *A Wilkie Collins Chronology* (Basingstoke, 2007)

Baker, William, and William M. Clarke, ed., *The Letters of Wilkie Collins* (Houndmills, 1999)

Baker, William, Andrew Gasson, Graham Law and Paul Lewis, ed., *The Public Face of Wilkie Collins: The Collected Letters* (London, 2005)

Clarke, William, *The Secret Life of Wilkie Collins* (Sparkford, 2004)

Gasson, Andrew, *Wilkie Collins: An Illustrated Guide* (Oxford, 1998)

Heller, Tamar, *Wilkie Collins and the Female Gothic* (New Haven, 1992)

Law, Graham and Andrew Maunder, *Wilkie Collins: A Literary Life* (Houndmills, 2008)

Lonoff, Sue, *Wilkie Collins and His Victorian Readers: A Study in the Rhetoric of Authorship* (New York, 1982)

Mangham, Andrew, ed., *Wilkie Collins: Interdisciplinary Essays* (Newcastle, 2007)

Nayder, Lillian, *Unequal Partners: Charles Dickens, Wilkie Collins, and Victorian Authorship* (Ithaca, 2002)

Nayder, Lillian, *Wilkie Collins: Twayne's English Author Series* (New York, 1997)

O'Neill, Philip, *Wilkie Collins: Women, Property and Propriety* (Basingstoke, 1988)

Page, Norman, ed., *Wilkie Collins: The Critical Heritage* (London, 1974)

Peters, Catherine, *The King of Inventors: A Life of Wilkie Collins* (New Jersey, 1991)

Pykett, Lyn, *The Sensation Novel: From* The Woman in White *to* The Moonstone (Tavistock, 1994)

Pykett, Lyn, *Wilkie Collins: Authors in Context Series* (Oxford, 2005)

Rance, Nicholas, *Wilkie Collins and Other Sensation Novelists: Walking the Moral Hospital* (Rutherford, 1991)

Robinson, Kenneth, *Wilkie Collins: A Biography* (London, 1951).

Sayers, Dorothy L., *Wilkie Collins: A Critical and Biographical Study*, ed. E.R. Gregory (Toledo, 1977)

Smith, Nelson and R.C. Terry, *Wilkie Collins to the Forefront: Some Reassessments* (New York, 1995)

Taylor, Jenny Bourne, *In the Secret Theatre of Home: Wilkie Collins, Sensation Narrative, and Nineteenth-Century Psychology* (Athens, Ohio, 1992)

Taylor, Jenny Bourne, ed., *The Cambridge Companion to Wilkie Collins* (Cambridge, 2006)

Thoms, Peter, *The Windings of the Labyrinth: Quest and Structure in the Major Novels of Wilkie Collins* (Athens, Ohio, 1992)

Biographical note

Melisa Klimaszewski is an Assistant Professor of English at Drake University, where she specialises in Victorian literature, critical race and gender studies, and the literature of South Africa. She is co-author of *Charles Dickens*, one of the inaugural biographies in the *Brief Lives* series, and she has edited several of Charles Dickens' collaborative Christmas numbers, restoring them to print in their entirety. She has also published essays on nineteenth-century wet nurses and nursemaids. In addition to a work in progress on racial mixture in Wilkie Collins' works, her current research theorises collaboration in the Victorian periodical press.

HESPERUS PRESS

Hesperus Press is committed to bringing near what is far – far both in space and time. Works written by the greatest authors, and unjustly neglected or simply little known in the English-speaking world, are made accessible through new translations and a completely fresh editorial approach. Through these classic works, the reader is introduced to the greatest writers from all times and all cultures.

For more information on Hesperus Press, please visit our website: **www.hesperuspress.com**